The Seventh Life

What I Learned Editing, Researching, and Republishing Yogananda's

Praecepta

Donald Castellano-Hoyt

D1522571

©Donald Castellano-Hoyt
San Antonio, Texas

April, 2018, 1ST Edition, revised

ISBN-13: 978-1719255455
ISBN-10: 1719255458

Amanuensis Press, San Antonio, Texas

Dedication page

To all Western seekers after truth

Table of Contents

Acknowledgments

Thanks must be given for the guidance I have received over the last 40 years of my Kriya association with the Self-Realization Fellowship. Without that august organization I would not have known about Yogananda.

One of Yogananda's 'right hand' people was Sri Nerode, Kriya minister and expositor of Yogoda concepts. Sri Nerode's son, Anil, to whom Yogananda also conferred the title of "Sri," lived for several years with Yogananda at Mother Center, receiving Kriya initiation at the age of four. Now a Professor of Mathematics at Cornell University, Dr. Nerode has given unstintingly of his time to me clarifying various issues I had regarding the relationship of his Father and Yogananda. Anil's generosity extends to the Self-Realization Fellowship and he continues to manifest unwavering courtesy to all whom he meets. I am fortunate to be able to call him 'friend.'

The Facebook site "Yogananda-YSS-SRF History II" continues to play a pivotal role in my research providing a treasure trove of old documents, letters, photographs, and videos related to the history of Yogananda and his Self-Realization Fellowship movement. I have found the discussions there quite frank and articulate regarding the social (i.e., outer) life of Yogananda and his followers. For the important role it plays I heartily thank its administrators, Martine Vanderpoorten and Robert Ardito for their vision, leadership and energetic investment in founding, participating in, and supervising this FB site.

Lastly I thank Swami Satyeswaranandaji for actually confirming with his scholarship what I had come to understand through my spiritual growth during the latter part of my 40 year sojourn with Self-Realization Fellowship (SRF, Inc.). His books *Mahamuni Babaji and His Legacy* and *The Holy Bible in the Light of Kriya Yoga* are those treasures that require oft consultation.

Foreword

In the seven incarnations following a successful suicide the devotee trods a path that inevitably brings the soul face-to-face with the same issues which caused the precipitous self-induced conclusion of one's previous journey. My efforts in this incarnation related to republication of all seven volumes of Yogananda's Praecepta brought me face-to-face with past guru-disciple issues, but in this, the seventh life, the results are happily different.

Those previous guru-disciple issues had to do with reports of the guru's immoral behavior. Unable to reconcile my expectations of perfect guru behavior, I concluded the relationship precipitously. That relationship however extends through many lifetimes until the disciple has found that for which his heart yearns. The guru-disciple relationship is one of friendship, and the guru takes on a huge responsibility for the disciple. So as I think of it now, the relationship wasn't concluded with the ending my own life.

The first clue I got about this came when reading Yogananda's accounts of his friendship with George Eastman. Yogananda acknowledges his awareness that Eastman would commit suicide . . . what finally struck my attention is that Yogananda did not interfere with the act.

That this is my own seventh life since leaving the guru became clear as I wrestled with the issues presented in early discipleship in this lifetime and with the obvious, if not glaring, lack of specific written guidance in the guru's published works. During forty years of the guru-disciple relationship in this life, my eyes opened through practice of the wisdom of Yogananda's oft-repeated encouragement to meditate, rather than just living by his written words.

All this came to a conclusion during my literary editorial efforts republishing the seven volumes of Yogananda's "Your Praecepta."

I am happy for the struggle of these seven lifetimes; SRF, Inc. devotees warned me of the 'bad' karma that would strike me as a result of republishing "His teachings." Indeed some of them complained that I would end up "changing his teachings," as "so many others have done." Thankfully my ignorance of the difference between good and bad karma aided me in following what I considered a right and "goodly" path.

This is written for your entertainment. Take it as such. Life is for the living of each act rather than for the fearing.

Preface

Republishing the Indian edition of the Praecepta became a sheer joy, especially seeing Yogananda's broad vision of and for the spiritual development of mankind. As I noted in one of the Editor's Notes working with his words brought his presence closer to me – especially that one Palm Sunday evening in 2016 when the aroma of Christ's presence permeated the house as I labored on that manuscript.

In the Praecepta are some of the most lofty, soaring expressions of spiritual prose I had ever seen – and especially what piqued my interest was that I had found none of it in the last 35 years of studying the Lessons provided since 1958 by the incorporated version of the Self-Realization Fellowship.

Don't get me wrong -- it was through the current version of the Lessons that I was introduced to the concepts of friendship, spiritual loyalty, "growing in grace" thru Yogic means. Those 1958 Lessons plus the most rudimentary attempts at meditation were what made my wife exclaim before the first six months of effort were completed, "You have become the husband I always wanted." SRF Magazine printed that story as a testimonial in one of its 2010 quarterly editions.

Reviewing those Praecepta lessons gave additional light on Yogananda's later *Autobiography of a Yogi* (AOY). A speaker often modifies a story during much repetition and I found that charming. It made me take a closer look at times at the *AOY* because the first few times I had read it I had glossed over "what did he mean" when he said various things. The Praecepta gave clarification to some of those remarks, yet when I pursued the meaning(s) I found myself at odds with the current SRF, Inc. narrative about Yogananda and his teaching.

Many of those *AOY* remarks will be explored in this book.

This book is about joy and truth. Enjoy.

Chapter 1. Editor's Notes on the Various Praecepta Steps

Anecdotally speaking I understand that the Praecepta came about from hand-recording Master's talks. He said on several occasions that he had written nothing in the Praecepta. This is interesting to an editor such as myself since I find many topics in the Praecepta taken word for word from various earlier magazine articles, *East-West, Inner Culture*, etc., and many of those were written by Yogananda.

I am aware of the role assigned by Master to Louise Royston to take excerpts from lectures he had given and articles he had written, and make a course of lessons out of them. Later on, of course, other lay disciples (such as Kamala Silva) edited and submitted talks they had heard and transcribed, preparing them for inclusion in the Praecepta. However in my extant manuscript the Praecepta folios all demonstrate a publishing location in India with editing there. The textual material supports these observations. In addition Master consistently told students to write the Indian headquarters in Daksineswar and/or Ranchi if guidance were necessary. They were to submit their exam answers there as well.

Note that on the final page (p. 14) of Praeceptum 181, he identifies Ranchi as the headquarters of Self-Realization Fellowship and urges students to "RESOLVE TO MAKE A PILGRIMAGE TO THE SELF-REALIZATION HEADQUARTERS AT RANCHI, AND YOGODA MATH AT DAKSINESWAR."

The two most common questions raised by devotees when hearing about this republication is Master's statement on the first page of each lesson "To Be Confidentially Reserved FOR MEMBER'S USE ONLY;" the other issue has to do with the copyright status.

Confidentiality

Yogananda answers the confidential issue in Lesson 181, " . . .THESE LESSONS MUST NOT BE LEFT AROUND WHERE INQUISITIVE EYES MIGHT READ AND RIDICULE THEM." Even today SRF, Inc. will not allow prisoners to subscribe to the lessons (presumably for the same reason). When a Texas prisoner attempted to subscribe to the current SRF, Inc. Lessons, he was simply told that SRF doesn't allow it. They gave no other reason.

SRF, Inc. gave me permission to teach this prisoner the 20-20-20 breathing technique. I instructed him in the 'Hong Sau' technique. The prisoner used them with excellent results; he sought meditation instruction from two other institutions however. I am privy to his spiritual experiences as he gave me written descriptions of them. He is now enrolled with SRF., Inc. Lessons, although he calls me 'guru.'

But do remember that one of the earliest and worst scandals occurred to Yogananda in Miami, Florida when a fear of violence was invoked as a reason to block Yogananda from teaching there. See the *Appendix of References* for the New York Times story. (Appendix Reference article #1)

Sister Gyanamataji acknowledges in a June 13, 1935, letter to Sri Nerode the problems he's running into with people demanding their money back at his lectures. She mentions that Miss Marckwardt (former campaign manager for Yogananda) had run into the same thing, because former students would pirate the lessons, offering them as their own. Sister even names a Dallas woman who is giving out the Kriya initiations. It's such an urgent situation that Sister is asking Sri Nerode to use air mail to get Mrs. Ivy's address to Sister so that Mother Center can deal with her. (In Appendix Reference, See "#17 Gyanamata's Letter to Sri Nerode about Hamid Bey, paragraphs 3 and 4)

Copyright

The copyright status is simple enough, since all Yogananda's written and published material are subject to the 1909 US Copyright law. At minimum more than 56 years have elapsed, meaning that the second copyright would have expired on all his material.

In the famous SRF, Inc. lawsuit against Ananda (206 F. 3d 1322 - Self-Realization Fellowship Church v. Ananda Church of Selfrealization [sic]) the three judge panel discussed that

"BECAUSE ALL OF THE COPIED WORKS WERE CREATED BEFORE 1978, THE COPYRIGHT ACT OF 1909 GOVERNS THE VALIDITY OF THE INITIAL COPYRIGHTS... THESE INITIAL STATUTORY COPYRIGHTS RAN FOR A 28 YEAR TERM..."

I mentioned 56 years just to be pedantic; none of Yogananda's heirs renewed his copyrights (his heirs and not SRF, Inc. were the only ones who could legally renew his copyrights).

Thus the "Your Praecepta" are in the public domain, as are all of Yogananda's books. In the chapter *Rationale for Republishing the Praecepta* I detail my rationale for republishing these teachings. In the chapter *"Amanuensis Examples from the Praecepta and SRF, Inc."* I present examples of scientific amanuensis (editing) principles (first as applied by SRF, Inc. in its 1983 remake of *Songs of the Soul* (now in public domain), and then I give examples of my own use of such principles.

In the meantime in this chapter I present a cursory review of my *Editor's Notes* on each of the Steps. Some end with references to further in-depth discussion in other chapters.

Editor's Notes, Step I of VII

Lesson 8 of Step 1 omits instructions for the energization exercises. The narrative given in *AOY* is that Yogananda had initiated a

"UNIQUE SYSTEM OF PHYSICAL DEVELOPMENT, ""YOGODA," WHOSE PRINCIPLES I HAD DISCOVERED IN 1916. REALIZING THAT MAN'S BODY IS LIKE AN ELECTRIC BATTERY, I REASONED THAT IT COULD BE RECHARGED WITH ENERGY THROUGH THE DIRECT AGENCY OF THE HUMAN WILL. AS NO ACTION, SLIGHT OR LARGE, IS POSSIBLE WITHOUT WILLING, MAN CAN AVAIL HIMSELF OF HIS PRIME MOVER, WILL, TO RENEW HIS BODILY TISSUES WITHOUT BURDENSOME APPARATUS OR MECHANICAL EXERCISES. I THEREFORE TAUGHT THE RANCHI STUDENTS MY SIMPLE "YOGODA" TECHNIQUES BY WHICH THE LIFE FORCE, CENTRED [SIC] IN MAN'S MEDULLA OBLONGATA, CAN BE CONSCIOUSLY AND INSTANTLY RECHARGED FROM THE UNLIMITED SUPPLY OF COSMIC ENERGY. THE BOYS RESPONDED

WONDERFULLY TO THIS TRAINING, DEVELOPING EXTRAORDINARY ABILITY TO SHIFT THE LIFE ENERGY FROM ONE PART OF THE BODY TO ANOTHER PART..." (Yogananda, Paramhansa. Autobiography of a Yogi (Reprint of Original 1946 Edition) (p. 156). Crystal Clarity Publishers - A. Kindle Edition.)

Yogananda tells of embarrassing Dr. Lewis (Yogananda's earliest American male disciple) by doing some of these exercises publicly in front of a police officer. I had always assumed that Yogananda was doing (even then) the current set of 38 exercises.

But then I found Yogananda's 1925 Yogoda or Tissue-Will System of Physical Perfection. The exercises given there (approximately 44 of them) are presumably the same as given at the Ranchi school; they are grouped also according to physical need (postural health, breathing, cardio health, weight loss etc.). So it is not clear to me when the current standard set of 38 exercises was established. Srimati Nerode observes as well that there was a time when they were not known as Energization Exercises. (Appendix Reference, articles #19 and #20)

However, what is extremely interesting to me is Yogananda's disclosure of the initial Kriya technique on page three of that book! But he doesn't call it that, instead contexting it as a breathing technique:

"13. VERY IMPORTANT: WHILE TAKING THE YOGODA EXERCISES CONNECTED WITH BREATHING, VIZ., FIGS. 2, 3, 26, 36, 37 (A, B) [SIC], AND SPINAL EXERCISE (A), INHALE AND EXHALE SLOWLY, AND WITH EASE TO THE FULL EXTENT, WITHOUT PUTTING TOO MUCH EFFORT ON THE CHEST AND DIAPHRAGM, AND MAKE A KIND OF SUPPRESSED (THOUGH DISTINCTLY AUDIBLE AND ROUNDED) GUTTURAL SOUND "AW," WHILE INHALING, AND "EE" WHILE EXHALING (MOUTH CLOSED ALL THE TIME). WITH THE HEAD ALMOST ERECT AND PRESSING THE UNDER SIDE OF THE CHIN SLIGHTLY AGAINST THROAT (NOT AGAINST THE CHEST), THOSE SOUNDS CAN EASILY BE MADE. PUTTING MORE ATTENTION ON THE MAKING OF THESE SOUNDS WITH THE HELP OF THE BREATH THAN ON THE BARE ACT OF BREATHING IN OR OUT HELPS GRADUAL AND SLOW INTAKE OF BREATH WHILE INHALING AND GRADUAL AND SLOW RELEASE OF IT WHILE EXHALING. THERE SHOULDN'T BE MUCH HEAVING OF THE CHEST. NEVER BREATHE IN OR OUT QUICKLY OR JERKILY. INHALATION AND EXHALATION SHOULD TAKE THE SAME LENGTH OF TIME (MAXIMUM, 30 SECONDS FOR EACH, TO BE ATTAINED GRADUALLY). BY A LITTLE PRACTICE YOU WILL GET THE BREATHING ALL RIGHT." (Yogananda, Swami. YOGODA OR TISSUE-WILL SYSTEM OF PHYSICAL PERFECTION (Kindle Locations 134-149). Unknown. Kindle Edition.)

If you look at Yogananda's later written *Kriya* instructions you will find much the same wording, "BY A LITTLE PRACTICE YOU WILL GET THE BREATHING ALL RIGHT." In previous discussion of keeping these teachings for confidential use, the disclosure of the Kriya technique as a breathing technique is (to me) astounding.

For instance, look at what Yogananda made Mildred Lewis do when she received Kriya from him. Her daughter Brenda publishes a copy of the handwritten notes Mildred took down as dictated to her by Yogananda himself. This Kriya pledge was signed by Mildred and Yogananda on Jan. 10, 1921. The fifth point of her pledge,

"5. IF I DIVULGE WITHOUT YOUR PERMISSION EXTREME MISERY WILL OVERTAKE ME ACCORDING TO NATURAL LAWS." (P. 380, TREASURES AGAINST TIME, BRENDA LEWIS ROSSER, BORREGO PUBLICATIONS, CA., 2ND EDITION, 2001.)

And then also Master warns in Praeceptum 177, page 132, "THIS LESSON IS STRICTLY FOR YOUR PERSONAL USE. ANY VIOLATION WILL DISTURB THE INNER HARMONY OF YOUR SPIRITUAL LIFE DUE TO CASTING SPIRITUAL PEARLS BEFORE UNAPPRECIATIVE EYES." P. 177 gives the advanced Kriyas 3 and 4 (the so-called "Astral Samadhi") "which is experienced through the correct practice of the Third and Fourth Initiations." In other places of the Praecepta (including Praeceptum 181) he states that the permission of the guru is necessary for publication of or sharing these Praecepta.

And yet in 1925 Yogananda is giving out the Kriya as a breathing technique! Breathtakingly interesting! I understand from a former SRF, Inc., monk, that Swami Bimalananda occasionally stated that Yogananda would give out copies of the *Kriya* initiations to the Hollywood Temple congregation without any formal ceremony, but that Yogananda stopped doing that when he realized that the congregants weren't bothering to practice the techniques (perhaps one may surmise they weren't reading them either).

Editor's Notes, Step II of VII

In the Step II I placed a disclaimer of medical claims on the *Table of Contents* page. The "Health Culture" sections certainly reflect the previous teachings here in America of 1) homeopathy (through the 1890's) and 2) Natural Hygiene. In my view these teachings should not be overlooked. Yogananda includes them in these

Praecepta because they too represent the teachings of the Master Minds of India. Nonetheless I placed the disclaimer as a way of avoiding the charge of practicing medicine without a license.

But wisdom's baby ought not to be "thrown out with the bath water!" In Step II Yogananda claims in the "Health Culture" teachings that keeping one's body in a slightly alkaline state (through proper diet) would prevent all sickness. The idea was introduced as well in the early 1930's by Nobel Prize winner German physiologist Dr. Otto Warburg, "Disease can't survive in an alkaline body." His Nobel Prize was for his discovery that cancer cells thrive in a non-oxygen environment. Hence providing the physical body with an alkaline oxygen-enhancing diet would help the body overcome (heal or stop) cancer.

In the summary of Lesson 31 the "Silence maker" is mentioned on p. 164. I found a hand drawn picture by Yogananda in a note. He also calls it "The Temple of Silence."

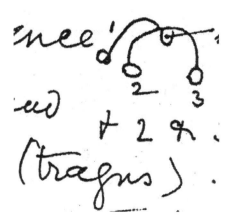

His note is to Sri Nerode,

"EVERY TIME YOU TEACH [THE] 5TH LESSON PLEASE LET ALL STUDENTS USE 'THE TEMPLE OF SILENCE.'
"NO. 1 GOES OVERHEAD &2 & 3 OVER THE EAR-LIDS (TRAGUS).
"INSTEAD OF USING THUMBS. [SIGNED] YOGANANDA"

Yogananda endorsed this apparatus to assist students in their practice of the "Om Technique" in addition to suggesting that the student close the tragus in each ear. I vaguely recall his writing somewhere that ear muffs may be utilized as well.

A fellow devotee and I used to wear earmuffs in our local group setting when practicing the *Aum* technique. But we stopped because so much consternation was raised by group members.

Here is an advertisement from one of the Inner Culture magazines:

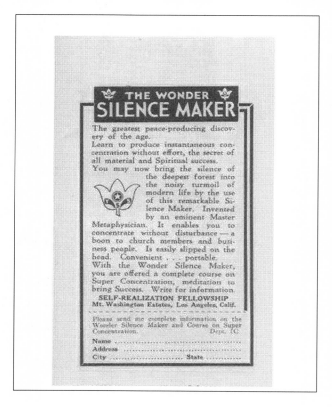

Several of the Praecepta of this Step reference "Paramhansa Swami" Yogananda. Master states in *Autobiography of a Yogi* that the Paramhansa honorific title supersedes the "Swami" title, and therefore replaces it. However, this anomaly appears to be sanctioned by the Master in its appearance here. I addressed this issue earlier.

For further discussion please see the chapter "Paramhansa Swami Yogananda."

Editor's Notes, Step III of VII

Preliminary Observations

This Step of my copy has more cover folios than the previous two steps. A review of these mailing covers reveals that they weren't mailed out (to this Indian student at least) in chronological order. Praecepta 58 - 101, and 113 - 148 show Rajasi Janakananda as President of Self-Realization Fellowship. Praeceptum 77 shows "Sister Daya" as President. And 78/3 shows Paramhansa Yogananda's name only, as Founder of Self-Realization Fellowship. The other Praecepta in this Step (as given to me) either have no folio or only the front page of the mailing folio.

Praeceptum 68 lists 12 items helpful for "Ideal Diets" of the yogi. Interestingly items "Nos. 6 to 8 [are] omitted for being unsuitable for Indian students." (Pgs 102-3 of Step III) The observation confirms that this copy of the Praecepta was solely published in India.

Obeservations

In prelude to a 1946 written Kriya initiation the following statement is made:

"IN 1934...SELF-REALIZATION FELLOWSHIP, THE WESTERN DIVISION OF YOGODA SAT-SANGA, INSTITUTED A NEW, REVOLUTIONIZING SYSTEM OF STUDY THROUGH THE MAILS, KNOWN AS "FORTNIGHTLY PRAECEPTA" WHICH ARE READ, DIGESTED AND ACCLAIMED BY THOUSANDS. THESE VITAL INSTRUCTIONS EMANATE EACH FORTNIGHT FROM THE SELF-REALIZATION FELLOWSHIP HEAD QUARTERS AT DAKSINESWAR, P. O. ARIADAH, DT. 24 PARGANAS, BENGAL, ASSURING EACH MEMBER OF EVER-PROGRESSIVE, EVER-ILLUMINATING INSPIRATION AND GUIDANCE - DESIGNED TO

CREATE KRISHNA-LIKE, LAHIRI MAHASAYA-LIKE SOULS IN THE SCIENTIFIC LABORATORY OF YOGODA, THAT WHICH IMPARTS YOGA, WITH THE SPECIMEN OF SELF. IT MAY BE NOTED THAT FOR STUDENTS IN EUROPE AND AMERICA THE YOGODA PRAECEPTA ARE ISSUED FROM THE WESTERN HEAD QUARTERS AT LOS ANGELES, CALIFORNIA."

It was to this I pointed the lawyers involved in copyright validation as I published each of the seven Praecepta volumes. There is no copyright on them, and of course the laws of India wouldn't necessarily appertain here; and even if they did, more than 56 years (US Copyright goes for 28 years and, when or if they are renewed for a second time for 28 years would equal 56 years) has elapsed.

Even now there are copyright apprentices with CreateSpace who still claim to me that Yogananda's early magazines (from 1925) are still under copyright protection. This occurs in-spite-of the Federal Judges (I think both Garcia and Brunetti) declaring these specific SRF, Inc. articles controlled by the 1909 US Copyright laws.

Editor's Notes, Step IV of VII

Preliminary Observations

At least two of Yogananda's beloved prayers are in this Step: "Prayer at Noon," and "God's Boatman." "Prayer at Noon" is available from SRF, Inc., as audio recordings.

OBSERVATIONS

In Praeceptum 96 Yogananda gives one of the finest exhortations for acknowledging God as the only doer.

"YOU ARE LIVING DIRECTLY BY THE POWER OF GOD. YOU ARE SUPPLIED DIRECTLY BY GOD. SUPPOSE GOD SUDDENLY CHANGED THE CLIMATE OF THIS COUNTRY. WHAT THEN? WHERE WOULD BE THE FOOD? HOW WOULD YOU LIVE? WHY NOT REMEMBER THAT GOD IS THE SUPPORTER OF THAT LIFE WHICH HE GAVE TO YOU? EVEN THOUGH HE MADE THAT LIFE DEPENDENT UPON FOOD, STILL HE IS THE DIRECT SUPPORT. HE IS THE CAUSE OF EVERYTHING, SO WHEN YOU LOSE YOUR CONNECTION WITH GOD YOU ARE BOUND TO SUFFER."

He doesn't use the actual words until the Summary of P. 96.

"The idea of business for private profiteering must cease. Business must evolve out of selfishness into service for one's fellow beings. Work with the consciousness that God is the Doer. All work is for Him. Learn to understand the law of order which governs our actions. Live simply, and live by a common principle, serving one another. It is selfishness that creates duality. In unselfishness, unity exists. God first, always. Become saturated in devotion and love for God. Sing always in your heart and that song will overflow into all of your life: "Spirit and Nature, Spirit and Nature. Victory to Spirit and Victory to Nature.""

I love that Yogananda does not get embroiled in the philosophic nuance of personal responsibility. He seems to be saying, 'give to Caesar what is Caesar's, and to God what is God's," i.e., God is the doer, but our action is necessary. In the quotations above Yogananda gives the basis of man's action, even though realizing God as the only "doer."

Read further discussion in the chapter, "God as the Only Doer."

Editor's Notes, Step V of VII

Preliminary Observations

Praeceptum -Page Two- (p. 129) This reading doesn't make sense:

"Under chloroform, your body does not feel the pain of a surgical operation, for the mind can consciously *to know* the condition of the body while under an operation, without feeling pain, which is created by one's hyper-sensitive awareness." The current SRF, Inc. Lesson makes sense: "Under chloroform, a surgical operation on the body is painless, for the mind is not aware of the condition of the body."

Yogananda makes an interesting observation about the future in P. 126 (p. 144):

"You, who are reading, and I, who am writing... will exist a hundred years hence only as thoughts." Yogananda occasionally remarked that the Praecepta was derived from his speeches rather than his writings. In at least one of the East-West magazines an article is marked as "transcribed by anonymous."

Yogananda's 'Prayer at Dawn' in Praeceptum has been released as an audio recording of his voice.

Observations

Even though Yogananda acknowledges that the teaching he brings is from the 'Master Minds' of India, he also points out that we are receiving Sriyukteswar's training that Yogananda received in his 14 years with him. "SO REMEMBER, THAT IS THE TEACHING YOU ARE RECEIVING. IF YOU PRACTICE THE TEACHING, IT WILL EMANCIPATE YOU BECAUSE IT IS FROM GOD." p. 74, Praeceptum 115.

I have often said over the last forty years that SRF, Inc. brings this message, but to realize that SRF, Inc. itself is not the message. Praeceptum 17 (p. 4) "SELF-REALIZATION FELLOWSHIP INSTRUCTION   TEACHES   YOU   THE   SCIENTIFIC   METHOD OF CONCENTRATION," Yogananda asserts.

That is why, in my view, that it was so important that SRF, Inc. sue Ananda Church of Self-Realization and lose that lawsuit. Presiding Federal Judge Edward J. Garcia ruled that SRF, Inc. did not own the term "Self-Realization" and this was upheld on appeal before a 3-judge panel. The final jury verdict in 2002 upheld this as well. Why is this important? Because before that judgment my assumption is that SRF, Inc. may have claimed that the designation "Self-Realization Fellowship Instruction" belongs to them and not to anyone else (such as me).

As I said earlier SRF, Inc. itself is not the message. And even though it is incorporated as a church in the State of California, it is ordained to carry the message,

"(D) TO TEACH A RELIGION OR PREACH A RELIGION KNOWN AS "SELF-REALIZATION FELLOWSHIP " (YOGODA SAT-SANGA), THE PRACTICAL AIM OF WHICH IS TO MAKE LASTING YOUTH AND ARREST OLD AGE BY USING THE UNLIMITED POWER OF GOD AND COSMIC ENERGY INSTEAD OF TRYING TO OBTAIN HEALTH ONLY FROM THE USE OF THE PHYSICAL MEANS OF FOOD AND EXERCISE . . ." (1935 Articles of Incorporation).

In this way SRF, Inc. avoids making itself the message or the arbiter of this message (in my humble opinion). I will write more about this in the chapter "Church Doctrine and Defamation of Yogananda's Disciples."

Editor's Notes, Step VI of VII

Preliminary Observations

The opening prayer of P-132 is read beautifully by Mrinalini Mataji in one of the recorded Christmas meditations she conducted.

Page three appears to be missing. The story of "John" the accountant is picked up at his sixth incarnation. Yogananda recites this story in one of SRF Inc.'s recordings.

Two Praeceptum 141, page 5, recipes actually show a serving of 2/4 portions of various ingredients. Intriguing . . .

"Exanthemata" (Page 4 of Praeceptum 142) is a reference to measles, rubella, childhood infectious diseases.

Observations

This Step delves into *karma* and reincarnation. Later in his *Autobiography of a Yogi*, points out a feature of the guru-disciple relationship that is quite interesting:

"[ELIJAH IS SPEAKING TO HIS DISCIPLE ELISHA] . . .NEVERTHELESS, IF THOU SEE ME WHEN I AM TAKEN FROM THEE, IT SHALL BE SO UNTO THEE.... AND HE TOOK THE MANTLE OF ELIJAH THAT FELL FROM HIM." 228 THE ROLES BECAME REVERSED, BECAUSE ELIJAH-JOHN WAS NO LONGER NEEDED TO BE THE OSTENSIBLE GURU OF ELISHA-JESUS, NOW PERFECTED IN DIVINE REALIZATION. (Yogananda, Paramhansa. Autobiography of a Yogi (Reprint of Original 1946 Edition) (p. 203). Crystal Clarity Publishers - A. Kindle Edition.)

In *The Incredible Life of a Himalayan Yogi The Times, Teachings and Life of Living Shiva: Baba Lokenath Brahmachari* (Shuddhaanandaa Brahmachari, Lokenath Divine Life Mission, Kolkata, India. Kindle Edition.)   a similar role reversal occurs in which Baba Lokenath, fully enlightened and freed of all three subtle body encumbrances while living, promises his less developed guru to seek him out and bring him in his guru's next lifetime to that sublime status to which his guru had helped Lokenath in this lifetime.

Upon the passing of several highly advanced disciples of Lokenath a kind of guessing game ensued among Lokenath's remaining disciples as to which of them had been Lokenath's guru. According to Swami Shuddhananda that was never revealed by Lokenath.

Whether or not Elijah (John the Baptist) needed further help from Elisha (Jesus of Nazareth) to re-attain his previous spiritual stature Yogananda only hints.

Yogananda states in "The Second Coming of Christ,"

"JESUS KNEW OF THE ABOVE LAW OF EMANCIPATION. HE MUST HAVE FOUND IN JOHN HIS REINCARNATED GURU, (A GURU, ALTHOUGH INFERIOR IN SPIRITUAL QUALITY, IS A GURU JUST THE SAME, A VEHICLE OF GOD ALWAYS). THIS IS WHY JESUS INSISTED ON BEING BAPTIZED BY JOHN THE BAPTIST. JESUS ALSO HAD SPOKEN OF JOHN THE BAPTIST AS THE REINCARNATED PROPHET, ELIAS (ELIJAH)."

Scripture implies that John the Baptist considered himself lower than Jesus.

Jesus said: "SUFFER IT TO   BE SO NOW, FOR THUS IT BECOMETH US TO FULFILL ALL RIGHTEOUSNESS." The Sanskrit Scriptures have a statement exactly parallel to this.

"THERE ARE MANY SAGES WITH MANY WISDOMS (SIC) WITH THEIR SCRIPTURAL AND SPIRITUAL INTERPRETATIONS, APPARENTLY CONTRADICTORY, BUT THE REAL SECRET OF RELIGION IS HIDDEN IN [THE] CAVE [OF THE SPIRITUAL EYE]." (Loc. Sit., Kindle Locations 187-191). UNKNOWN. Kindle Edition.)

Editor's Notes, Step VII of VII

Early in this book I extolled the lofty expressions of Yogananda in the Praecepta which I had not found in SRF, Inc.'s version of the lessons.

Praeceptum 181 (include 179 here as well, if you like)

"ALL OF YOU WHO HAVE GONE THROUGH THE SEVEN STEPS CAN ACT AS PRECEPTORS TO TEACH OTHER TRUTH-THIRSTY SOULS, OR OPEN GROUPS, IN YOUR OWN HOMES OR TO START CENTERS (AFFILIATED WITH THE HEAD-QUARTERS) FOR LIBERATING OTHERS, YOU HAVE WANTED LIBERATION NOT ONLY FOR YOURSELF BUT FOR OTHERS. A SOUL CANNOT BE LIBERATED UNLESS HE HELPS OTHERS TO LIBERATE THEMSELVES THROUGH SELF-REALIZATION METHODS. IT IS YOUR BOUNDEN DUTY TO REMEMBER TO PRACTICE ALL YOU HAVE LEARNED IN YOUR DAILY LIFE AND THROUGHOUT YOUR OWN LIFE. THE MORE YOU PRACTICE, THE BETTER FITTED YOU WILL BE TO HELP LIBERATE OTHERS . . . [I]N THIS PATH, ALL WHO HAVE GONE THROUGH THE SEVEN STEPS CAN ACT AS PRECEPTORS TO OTHERS, BUT ONLY BY YEARS OF MERGING IN THE TRUTH CAN HE ULTIMATELY ATTAIN THE PARAMHANSA STATE. FROM THAT STATE ON, GOD DIRECTLY HANDLES THE LIFE OF THE DEVOTEE." (YOGANANDA, PARAMHANSA. YOUR PRAECEPTA: VII (KINDLE LOCATIONS 3213-3220). UNKNOWN.)

This excerpt is pregnant with possibilities for spiritually mature, realized souls. I lift here the one concept for discussion that is of most value to me:

"A SOUL CANNOT BE LIBERATED UNLESS HE HELPS OTHERS TO LIBERATE THEMSELVES THROUGH SELF-REALIZATION METHODS."

This is the only place I have ever heard or seen Yogananda quoted as stating this truth. Anecdotally I have always heard that the devotee must help liberate at least six others before that devotee can be finally liberated.

On the face of it, of course, the math is impossible, i.e., those six candidates for your help must also each help liberate six others, etc., etc. So as Yogananda does with Edwin Arnold's translation of Krishna's famous statement "only one in a million who seeks me, find me" I will take the liberty of pointing out that it's not a mathematical game, but a way of selfless service.

We know that Gyanamataji had disciples, and for sure, Yogananda said of her that she had achieved liberation "without experiencing the bliss" in this lifetime.

Anecdotally I understand that Rajarsi's Japanese gardener was his disciple.

In video tape Daya Mataji says that she won't be anyone's guru; and does so in the context that there is only one guru, i.e., her Yogananda.

An SRF *gurubhai* tells me that he didn't want to receive *diksha* from Swami Kriyananda, so he moved down the California coast to embrace Yogananda through SRF, Inc. pretty much along the lines that (I think) Daya Ma indicated above. Nonetheless Kriyanandaji has disciples; I am not one of them, but I am happy that a couple months prior to his death he forgave me for my rudeness to him (which I do not discuss here). I thoroughly enjoyed his generosity towards me in those final months in his communications through his secretary Lakshman.

Here is an email I sent to Lakshman back in March of 2013,

"KRIYANANDAJI'S FAITHFULNESS TO OUR GURU IS WHAT "WON ME OVER," SO TO SPEAK. I TOLD A FRIEND . . . (FORMER POSTULANT WITH SRF) THAT OVER THE LAST 18 MONTHS I HAVE CHANGED IN MANY WAYS, AND ONE OF THEM IS THAT WHATEVER OF KRIYANANDA'S THAT I READ, I SENSE MASTER'S PRESENCE. SINCE MASTER APPEARED IN MY SPIRITUAL EYE LAST YEAR ON SRI YUKTESWAR'S MAHASAMADHI HIS PRESENCE HAS BEEN PRONOUNCED. I AM ALWAYS GRATEFUL WHEN GURUJI DRAWS ME TO THOSE OF HIS OWN WHO LOVE HIM LIKE I DO."

"MAY YOUR DAYS CONTINUE TO BE FILLED WITH BLISS, KRIYANANDAJI, AND PLEASE KNOW THAT I LOVE AND APPRECIATE YOU WITH DIVINE LOVE AND APPRECIATION PURGED AND CLEANSED BY THE FAITHFULNESS OF OUR GURU!"

In the chapter regarding Yogananda's and SRF, Inc.'s handling of disciples I will discuss what appears to me to be the ongoing character assassination of Kriyananda by SRF, Inc.

Some of Yogananda's disciples that had disciples include the following:

1. Kamala Silva (the first female lay person Yogananda ordained outside the structure of SRF, Inc.)
2. Durga Ma (Mrs. Florina Alberta Dufour Darling)
3. Yogacharya Black
4. Mother Hamilton
5. Roy Eugene Davis
6. Swami Kriyanandaji
7. Swami Premanandaji
8. Sri Nerode
9. Swami Dhiranandaji
10. Swami Atmanandaji (the former Prabhas Chandra Ghose, Yogananda's nephew)
11. Swami Satchidanandaji of YSS and Ranchi (one of his female disciples became a paramhansa shortly after her birth)
12. Swami Bidyanandaji of YSS and Ranchi
13. Yogacharya Cuaron

and many others whose names I do not know.

And each of us will, in the course of our spiritual maturation, take on disciples. Yogananda teaches in the Praecepta that God is the one who calls, ordains the guru. But when you combine that truth with the greater truth that 'God is the guru' then regardless of your level of spiritual attainment God is in charge.

In the chapter "Church Doctrine and Defamation of Yogananda's Disciples" I will discuss personality issues and continuation of defamation of several of these Yogananda disciples.

Chapter 2. Rationale for Republishing the Praecepta

"DO NOT ACCEPT BLINDLY WHAT I SAY; PRACTICE AND PROVE FOR YOURSELVES FROM YOUR OWN EXPERIENCE." Kamala (Silva) quotes Yogananda in her book, *The Flawless Mirror*, (copyright renewed 1992).

At the end of the Praecepta (P. 181) are found these very encouraging words,

"FINISHING THE SEVEN STEPS GIVES YOU THE CERTIFICATE SO THAT YOU CAN HELP OTHERS SPIRITUALLY AND SPREAD THE CAUSE OF SELF-REALIZATION THROUGH YOUR EXAMPLE AND TEACHING . . . YOU MUST FEEL THAT GOD AND THE GREAT GURUS WILL BE TEACHING AND HELPING OTHERS THROUGH YOU, AND YOU MUST REGARD EVERYONE AS A TEMPLE OF GOD EVEN THOUGH THAT INDIVIDUAL IS NOT CONSCIOUS OF HIM. ALWAYS PRAY, 'HEAVENLY FATHER, MAY THY LOVE SHINE FOREVER ON THE SANCTUARY OF MY DEVOTION, AND MAY I BE ABLE TO AWAKEN THY LOVE IN TRUTH-THIRSTY HEARTS'. . .YOU MUST SHARE YOUR SELF-REALIZATION BY INTERESTING OTHERS IN THIS PATH . . . PLEASE REMEMBER . . . TO BE THE INSTRUMENT TO IMPART SELF-REALIZATION AND GOD CONSCIOUSNESS TO OTHERS IS THE GREATEST BOON. . . REMEMBER, YOU COULD NOT GET THE TRUTH UNLESS THE MASTERS GAVE IT TO YOU THROUGH PRAECEPTA TEACHINGS . . . YOU CAN TEACH EVERY MEMBER OF THE GROUP YOU START, THE CONCENTRATION AND MEDITATION LESSON AND THE TENSION EXERCISES, AND READ TO THE GROUP A PART OF YOUR PRAECEPTA. . .WRITE TO HEAD-QUARTERS ... IN REGARD TO WHATEVER ACTIVITIES YOU TAKE UP FOR THE PURPOSE OF ATTAINING SELF-REALIZATION. . .WITH UNCEASING BLESSINGS,"
[SD] PARAMHANSA YOGANANDA

For 40 years of my discipleship I have heard references to Yogananda's Praecepta -- sometimes in hushed reverential terms ...but no one seemed to have access to them.

Thankfully for me a Facebook friend made a PDF Xeroxed Indian copy available to me in 2016. Immediately enthralled with the religious fervor oozing from the various Praecepta, I wanted to make them available once again in print. They would perhaps put into perspective Yogananda's original teaching and/or intent . . . maybe . . . maybe not.

For example Yogananda says in *Autobiography of a Yogi*

"THE NEXT AFTERNOON, WITH A FEW SIMPLE WORDS OF BLESSING, SRIYUKTESWAR BESTOWED ON ME THE FURTHER MONASTIC TITLE OF PARAMHANSA. 'IT NOW FORMALLY SUPERSEDES YOUR FORMER TITLE OF SWAMI,' HE SAID AS I KNELT BEFORE HIM." [YOGANANDA, PARAMHANSA. AUTOBIOGRAPHY

OF A YOGI (REPRINT OF ORIGINAL 1946 EDITION) (P. 250). CRYSTAL CLARITY PUBLISHERS - A. KINDLE EDITION.].

When I read that forty years ago as a new student, I assumed that 'swami' was not to be used in addressing him, and even thought it a doctrinal issue. But there on page 2 of Praeceptum 2: "PARAMHANSA SWAMI YOGANANDA RECEIVED HIS TITLE OF "SWAMI" AND "PARAMHANSA" FROM HIS GREAT MASTER, SWAMI SREE-YUKTESWAR GIRIJI MAHARAJA OF BENGAL..." and then the combined titles were used not only in later Praecepta but on several of the mailing covers as well.

I googled the combined terms and found them in common use in India; surprisingly it dawned on me that Sriyukteswar's disciple Sailendra Bejoy Dasgupta titled his biography of Yogananda, *Paramhansa Swami Yogananda: Life-portrait and Reminiscences.* [Dasgupta, Sri Sailendra Bejoy. Paramhansa Swami Yogananda: Life-portrait and Reminiscences . Yoga Niketan, Inc.. Kindle Edition.]

Both Sriyukteswar and Yogananda insist that a devotee's 'eyes of reason' must not be put out just because he or she has undertaken the disciple/guru relationship. I have found other issues that bear another "look," for example, how many gurus does a devotee need?

Additionally I republished the Praecepta to take away the guesswork from devotees and interested parties who otherwise have only snippets of the Praecepta on which to base their opinion about the spiritual stature of these teachings. It is important here to note that one of the issues settled in the 12 year legal battle between SRF, Inc. and Ananda Church of Self-Realization is that talking about Yogananda and his teachings is entirely different from talking about SRF, Inc. That is, a "knock" on Yogananda is not a "knock" on SRF, Inc. If in this book I seem to say anything negative about Yogananda (for instance), according to judicial findings and findings of the jury in that celebrated lawsuit, [(206 F.3d 1322 (9th Cir. 2000)] I am not thereby defaming SRF, Inc.

Self-Realization Fellowship minister Kamala Silva lamented upon seeing the SRF, Inc. 1956 rewrite of these Praecepta into the current SRF Lessons, allegedly said, "they are ruining the pristine words of my guru!" I leave it to every person who reads the Praecepta to keep their eyes of reason and their receptivity of hope and love open to the ministrations of that gurudev who uttered the words recorded therein.

Ironically now that the original Praecepta are reprinted, SRF, Inc. has announced that sometime in the near future (perhaps 2018) SRF, Inc. will publish a new rendition of the lessons with more detail and clarifications especially of Kriya practice. A friend (a former SRF monk) laughingly suggested to me that SRF, Inc. is publishing a new rendition of its lessons simply in response to republication of the original Praecepta. I heartily dismissed the idea, but it was worth a nice laugh!

Chapter 3. Examples of Amanuensis from SRF, Inc. and Me

On the other hand let us be clear about editing of Yogananda's writings. The editorial principles I employed is called amanuensis, and is historically used by Biblical linguistic experts when trying to reconstruct a text (say from a parchment) that has enough of the text intact at the expected points so that the linguists can confidently match the existing "dots and tittles" with the predictable Hebrew or Greek text so that the original can be reconstructed.

SRF, Inc. used amanuensis in its detailed narrative of their 1983 republication of Yogananda's Songs of the Soul.

Here is SRF, Inc.'s 1983 amanuensis of "Songs of the Soul."

"PUBLISHER'S NOTE

"IT IS WITH DEEP SATISFACTION THAT WE OFFER THIS TREASURY OF POEMS BY PARAMAHANSA YOGANANDA. THE PRESENT VOLUME FULFILLS A LONG-STANDING DESIRE TO RESTORE TO PRINT THOSE POEMS OF HIS THAT WERE PUBLISHED IN EARLIER YEARS UNDER THE TITLE SONGS OF THE SOUL, AND TO BRING TOGETHER UNDER THAT TITLE MANY OF PARAMAHANSAJI'S OTHER POEMS FROM VARIOUS SELF-REALIZATION PUBLICATIONS, PAST AND PRESENT.

"CONSIDERABLE THOUGHT AND RESEARCH HAVE GONE INTO THE PREPARATION OF THIS EDITION. ORIGINAL WRITINGS AND TRANSCRIPTS WERE COMPARED WITH VARIANT RENDERINGS INTRODUCED BY EARLY EDITORS, AND BY PARAMAHANSAJI HIMSELF; FOR HE WOULD SOMETIMES PEN CORRECTIONS AND CREATIVE VARIATIONS THAT CAME TO HIM WHEN REREADING A POEM, OR INTERPOLATE A FRESH INSPIRATION WHILE RECITING A PASSAGE IN THE COURSE OF A LECTURE OR DEVOTIONAL SERVICE. THE NUMBER OF SUCH VARIATIONS IN A POEM IS GENERALLY PROPORTIONATE TO THE FREQUENCY OF ITS USE. IN MANY CASES THEY ARE SLIGHT—A MORE PRECISE WORD, A DIFFERENT TURN OF PHRASE, OCCASIONALLY A DELETION (OR ADDITION) OF A THOUGHT, OR OF CERTAIN LINES, TO FIT A PARTICULAR CONTEXT. THE PRESENT ENDEAVOR HAS BEEN TO ADHERE TO PARAMAHANSAJI'S ORIGINAL HANDWRITTEN OR SPOKEN VERSION; AND FROM THE MODIFICATIONS HE INTRODUCED, TO RETAIN THOSE THAT SUBSTANTIALLY CLARIFY HIS THOUGHT OR OTHERWISE ADD TO THE BEAUTIFUL IMAGERY OF HIS INSPIRATION.

"WE WERE HAPPY TO FIND AND RESTORE NOT ONLY ILLUSTRATIVE WORDS AND PHRASES, BUT ALSO ENTIRE LINES OR STANZAS THAT HAD BEEN OMITTED FROM THESE POEMS WHEN THEY WERE ORIGINALLY PUBLISHED. THE FOLLOWING ARE A FEW EXAMPLES:

"In the selection, Flower Offering, some of the phrases omitted or changed in the first version printed in 1923, and now restored in this new edition are *devotion-sweetened musk*

"("devotion-sweetened musk" instead of "devotion's perfume")

*with silent song in me
I come to worship Thee*

"("With silent song in me" — this line was omitted — "I come to worship Thee")

"An entire new stanza has been added. Written in rough draft by Paramahansaji, but never printed:

*For naught from Thee I pray or long
That I bring offerings song
I want just to tell
In secret what I feel*

"("For naught from Thee I pray or long That I bring offering and song. I just want to tell In secret what I feel.")

"In Thy Homecoming, "the steady sentinels" was misread and printed originally as "speedy sentinels":

*The steady sentinels of
are patiently waiting for Thy home
coming*

"("The steady sentinels of sun and moon are patiently waiting for Thy homecoming").

"In A Mirror New, the word "loyal" had been omitted:

would loyal show, all true

"("Would loyal show, all true").

"The charming line,

"("Ere the sorcerer Sleep doth call"), had also been left out.

"In At the Roots of Eternity, several unused descriptive words and phrases from the original handwritten copy were restored, such as:

"("with singing leaves, " instead of "swaying trees")

"("with bounding planet-balls," instead of "whirling planets")

"("nectar loot, " which had not been included).

"In Listen to My Soul Song, possibly the editor could not make out the handwritten word "gloaming,"

"("Beneath the gloaming of dim devotion of eyes unseeing").

"It was originally printed as "gloom of dim devotion." That first printing also omitted the phrase "of eyes unseeing."

"Similar corrections and restorations were made in many of the other poems as well, such as the addition in Variety of two previously unpublished stanzas at the end, and the picturesque phrase

"("Thy debut, O Eternity").

"With this scanning of original manuscripts and transcriptions, we feel we have accomplished the review of these poems that Paramahansaji had started, but did not have time to finish. Since in many cases there was more than one "original" or "approved" version, we have chosen for this edition the rendering most often recited by Paramahansaji himself. Where such evidence was lacking, we selected those words or phrases deemed most characteristic   of his unique mode of expression — as cited in the foregoing examples."

Castellano-Hoyt Accurate Amanuensis of a Missing Page

In the Editor's Notes for the Summary Lessons of Step I (One) I lamented the loss of the final page of the summary of Praeceptum 21 [Praeceptum No. 26/3, Page 6].

My Indian copy goes as far as "If the breath stays in, wait; otherwise, as soon... "

By extrapolating from previous Summary patterns and consulting the current SRF, Inc. summary, I reconstituted the text as follows in the left column. Recently I found the missing half page. Compare how closely the reconstituted amanuensis efforts (left column) echo the original (right column):

as the breath goes out quickly or slowly, all the way, mentally, say, without sound or whisper or use of the lips or tongue, "Sau." Repeat each sound as instructed with each corresponding incoming and outgoing breath.	as the breath goes on quickly or slowly, all the way, mentally, say, without sound or whisper or use of the lips or tongue, "Hong", 6) if the breath stays in, wait; otherwise as soon as the breath comes out quickly or slowly, all the way mentally say without sound or whisper or use of the lips or tongue, "Sau". If the breath stays out, wait otherwise when it goes in slowly quickly, all the way mentally chant "Hong", and when the breath comes out quickly or slowly, (or its own accord without force of act of will) mentally chant "Sau" all the way. Keep repeating the above as long as you w ant to do so. In this way you keep your attention repeated to one thing at a time, the breath and in so doing you separate yourself from the breath, thus realizing th at you are not the body, not the breath, but you are the consciousness and intelligence in the body. You are a soul.

THE MEANING OF HONG SAU

"Hong" is the vibration of the incoming breath; "Sau" is the vibration of outgoing breath. Conscious chanting of the words together quiets the breath, as that is the breath's astral vibration. Continued practice of the technique enables the yogi to experience himself as separate from the body and breathing. He then is able to behold himself as the soul.

Q. What is the meaning of "Hong" and "Sau"?
Ans. "Hong" is the vibration of the in going breath. "Sau" is the vibration of the outgoing breath. Just as the word "Peace" produces calm ness in the mind and body, and as the word "Anger" vibrates breath, so also the chanting of "Hong" and "Sau" calms the breath quickly as that is its Astral vibration.

WHAT IS SLEEP

In sleep, we experience, voluntary, unconscious sensory relaxation. In death, complete relation involuntarily takes place, due to the stopping of the heart's action. If one can learn to control the heartbeat, he can experience the conscious death, leaving and re-entering the body at will; many Yogis of India, who have practiced "Hong-Sau" have, through it, achieved mastery over the action of the heart. Such Yogis have learned to leave the body voluntarily, honorably, and gladly, and are not thrown out roughly, or taken by surprise by death, when their lease on their body-temples expires.

Q. What is sleep?
Ans. Unconscious sensory motor relaxation, in which the life force and consciousness are unconsciously switched off from the lamp of the muscles and the senses.
Q. What does it mean "to die daily"?
Ans. By self-realization technique, as mentioned by St. Paul in Corinthians, this clause means to consciously switch off the life energy from the bodily lamp into the dynamo of spirit, or switch on the life force again into the body bulb.

BEST TIMES TO MEDITATE

The four times of change in the body during the day correspond to the four seasons. The purpose of this Lesson is to realize the changeless in the four changing periods of the body, by vitalizing and magnetizing it with Life Currents and Cosmic Consciousness.

These Currents arrest change and suspend the decay in the cells. Therefore, it is best to practice the changeless-producing Lessons four times a day for sure scientific results. Meditate between 5 and 6 A.M; 11 and 12 A.M.; 5 and 6 P.M.; 10 and 12 P.M.; or 11 and 12 P. M.

BEST TIME TO MEDITATE

Meditate half an hour or one hour any time between 6 to 8 AM or 10 to 2 PM or 5 to 8 PM or one hour or longer anytime between 9 PM to 1 AM.

If you cannot meditate four times a day, meditate twice in the morning and once before going to bed at night, and during leisure hour when lying down.

Certainly no meaning was lost nor changed through this application of amanuensis principles.

Where wording was at times difficult to translate, I appealed to other articles. For instance, the line that reads in my manuscript "Truancy of fleas" [actually published in one MS Word document I found online] is found correctly articulated in a poem as "truant flesh." (Praeceptum 16, p. 1, "In Stillness Dark") Here is a picture of it with 'flesh' misspelled:

```
               IN STILLNESS DARK
Hark!
In stillness dark,
When noisy dreams have slept,
The house is gone to rest,
And busy life
Doth cease from strife, --
The Soul in pity soft doth kiss
The Truant fless to soothe, and speak
With mind-transcending grace
Its soundless voice of peace.
```

I noted in context one impossible line having to do with putting "felons in lemon." I assume Yogananda was saying to add a lemon peel to a lemon drink, but I did not presume to correct the copy thus. (Praeceptum 19, p. 6). I recently discovered that the Amrita Foundation published it as "put a felon into lemon when there is a wound."

There is one interesting line that current SRF, Inc. Lessons read to this day as "Approach God with a Song of Smiles." (Praeceptum 26/3, page 3). The context (i.e., Praeceptum 19) however has everything to do with approaching God in the mirror of silence that we put up as we meditate. Since enough words and letters are available to justify a different reading, I have presumed to read the line as "Approach God with the Mirror of Silence."

Although anecdotes abound of mimeographing and changing the individual Praecepta at Mother Center, the reality I find in the original surviving manuscript I used confirmed the anecdotes in the breach! The over-typing of letters, dyslexic and haplographic errors and spellings, along with India-British spelling intermixed with American-English spelling, overuse of commas, and unpredictable capitalization of words — what a messy set of pages some students received as their lessons. Here is a sample:

S-I * P,6

YOGODA SAT-SANGA FORTNIGHTLY INSTRUCTIONS
BY
PARAMHANSA YOGANANDA
-oo-
(To be confidentinlly Reserved FOR MEMBER'S USE ONLY)

Chapter 4. American Philosophy and the Issue of Identity

An SRF friend years ago informed me by letter that he had quit practice of Kriya techniques because it did not give him the same beauty that he experiences with anal intercourse. I couldn't disagree with him; his experience is his. Ironically I too have stopped Kriya practice for a similar reason: it never produced the beauty in the last 40 years that the 'hong sau' technique and the manasa laya mantra produce.

My SRF friend identifies himself both as a soul and as gay; though I have never heard him invoke the attribution philosophy commonly espoused in America today, i.e., the attribution of "transgender" status, that persons thinking, believing, or feeling themselves to be a sexual gender are that emotive gender in spite of contrary biological and anatomical indications.

Years ago an 8 year old Jewish girl proclaimed to me upon our introduction that she is not Jewish and never would be. About four years later she repeated this astounding assertion, and her Jewish mother still had no answer for her daughter's persistent denial of her cultural and racial heritage.

However the experiences of both my friends are understandable from the standpoint of reincarnation. One of the truths inculcated among seekers after truth in India is that we attract to ourselves our deepest loves and our deepest hates. The role of reincarnation is to assist each soul to understand that we are only playing passing roles but everlastingly we are souls seeking perfect expression.

In his discussion of the concept and reality of reincarnation and its history of cultural and political rejection by the early Christian church, Yogananda points out, ". ...TRUTHS SUPPRESSED LEAD DISCONCERTINGLY TO A HOST OF ERRORS." (Autobiography of a Yogi, Cp. 16)

In the 1987 documentary film about the Jains of India moderated by Lindsey Wagner a segment points out that the outer façade of most Hindu temples is adorned with depictions of every conceivable sexual activity. There is no judgment pronounced on any activity; the point is that life on the outside of the temple is for outer physical union; and life inside the temple is for inner spiritual union with Spirit which is sexless. (Ahimsa: Non-Violence; 1987)

Yogananda gives an excellent example in this distinction by the Indian saint Ananda Moy Ma:

"MY CONSCIOUSNESS HAS NEVER ASSOCIATED ITSELF WITH THIS TEMPORARY BODY. BEFORE I CAME ON THIS EARTH, FATHER, 'I WAS THE SAME.' AS A LITTLE GIRL, 'I WAS THE SAME.' I GREW INTO WOMANHOOD, BUT STILL 'I WAS THE SAME.' WHEN THE FAMILY IN WHICH I HAD BEEN BORN MADE ARRANGEMENTS TO HAVE THIS BODY MARRIED, 'I WAS THE SAME.' AND WHEN . . . MY HUSBAND CAME TO ME . . . LIGHTLY TOUCHING MY BODY, HE RECEIVED A VIOLENT SHOCK, AS IF STRUCK BY LIGHTNING, FOR EVEN THEN 'I WAS THE SAME.'

"MY HUSBAND KNELT BEFORE ME, FOLDED HIS HANDS, AND IMPLORED MY PARDON . . . "EVEN WHEN I QUIETLY ACCEPTED THIS [FROM] MY HUSBAND . . ., 'I WAS THE SAME.' AND, [YOGANANDA], IN FRONT OF YOU NOW, 'I AM THE SAME.' . . .'" (YOGANANDA, PARAMHANSA. AUTOBIOGRAPHY OF A YOGI (REPRINT OF ORIGINAL 1946 EDITION) (P. 283). CRYSTAL CLARITY PUBLISHERS - A. KINDLE EDITION.)

And in an opposite vein Jewish scripture gives the account of Balaam and his talking donkey in Numbers 22:30ff: [Balaam was up to no good and the donkey (seeing the avenging angel that Balaam could not see) swerved into the side of the mountain apparently crushing Balaam's leg (thus saving Balaam's life)]

"...29 THEN BALAAM SAID TO THE DONKEY, "BECAUSE YOU HAVE MADE A MOCKERY OF ME! IF THERE HAD BEEN A SWORD IN MY HAND, I WOULD HAVE KILLED YOU BY NOW." 30THE DONKEY SAID TO BALAAM, "AM I NOT YOUR DONKEY ON WHICH YOU HAVE RIDDEN ALL YOUR LIFE TO THIS DAY? HAVE I EVER BEEN ACCUSTOMED TO DO SO TO YOU?" AND HE SAID, "NO." 31THEN THE LORD OPENED THE EYES OF BALAAM, AND HE SAW THE ANGEL OF THE LORD STANDING IN THE WAY WITH HIS DRAWN SWORD IN HIS HAND; AND HE BOWED ALL THE WAY TO THE GROUND...."

Yogananda and other Master Minds of India point out that occasionally a person indulging in a highly sensual animalistic way may have to be incarnated into an animal's body in order to safely work off all the animalistic instincts without garnering more human karma. Yogananda refers to examples of dogs that can count, animals that can talk, etc. He is clear that this is a rare occasion.

A person with an antipathy towards any particular group may find itself born into that group in its next incarnation as a way of broadening its understanding. A slave owner may find himself born as a slave, in order to work off his karmic burden of hate towards people of a different racial or political group from his own.

I do not know if my young Jewish friend will ever reconcile being Jewish with her racial heritage. In terms of the sociological discussion today, the girl may think of herself as a gentile trapped in a Jewish body!

That brings me to my real point, and that is the observation Yogananda attributes to his Swami, Sri Yukteswar.

""IN SLEEP, YOU DO NOT KNOW WHETHER YOU ARE A MAN OR A WOMAN," HE SAID. "JUST AS A MAN, IMPERSONATING A WOMAN, DOES NOT BECOME ONE, SO THE SOUL, IMPERSONATING BOTH MAN AND WOMAN, HAS NO SEX. THE SOUL IS THE PURE, CHANGELESS IMAGE OF GOD." (CP. 12, AUTOBIOGRAPHY OF A YOGI)

The Christians will never find a theological response to this metaphysical discussion simply because of rejecting the notion of reincarnation. In my view the Christian construct of a hostage-making, hostage-taking God must change. Christians believe in a God who sends souls to everlasting hell if they don't accept a "Stockholm syndrome" status (i.e., you are so good, God, I'll be good – just don't hurt me!).

My point is that Western philosophers have a responsibility to address the identity issue (i.e., sexual or racial or vocational, etc.) on rational grounds rather than on the passing political winds fueled by emotions. To my knowledge this is not being discussed in Western university philosophy classes.

Life is for the living, not fearing! Each person's desires are different; each will seek beauty in the way that seems best to them; no one else can experience for anyone else. That is the 'real' work.

Chapter 5. Paramhansa Swami Yogananda

I have noted in a previous chapter that several of the Praecepta reference "Paramhansa Swami" Yogananda. Master states in *Autobiography of a Yogi* that the Paramhansa honorific title supersedes the "Swami" title, and therefore replaces it. However, this anomaly appears to be sanctioned by the Master in its appearance here.

For me it was a doctrinal issue for nearly forty years until I read these wider usages. Other titles do not diminish Yogananda's spiritual attainment, even though SRF, Inc. continues to insist that adding the extra 'a' to param'a'hansa acknowledges Yogananda's spiritual stature! In all the descriptions of mystic encounters with him by several other disciples (Swamis Bidyanandaji and Satchidanandaji, as well as Yogananda's childhood friend Swami Satyanandaji) reference is rarely made to the param'a'hansa honorific, only 'Yogananda' or 'Master' is used; otherwise they spell the title interchangeably. I found a sample paragraph of this type of interchange in Satchidanandaji's description of becoming a swami:

"PARAMAHANSA YOGANANDAJI INITIATED ME INTO SWAMI ORDER IN A NON- CEREMONIAL (BIDWAT) WAY. HE HAD SELECTED MY RENUNCIATE NAME, YOGI SATCHIDANANDA GIRI. HE PLANNED TO GIVE THE RENUNCIATE'S ROBE IN 1951 WHICH I EAGERLY WAITING FOR. BUT HE COULD NOT COME TO INDIA.

"HE LEFT HIS MORTAL BODY ON 7TH MARCH, 1952. I ACCEPTED THE ROBE OF RENUNCIATION OFFICIALLY FROM SWAMI ATMANANDA GIRI ON 25TH APRIL, 1955. IN FACT, I THOUGHT OF NOT ACCEPTING THE ROBE FROM ANY ONE. BUT PEOPLE WOULD NOT RECOGNISE ME AS A SWAMI IF I DID NOT ACCEPT THE RENUNCIATE ROBE FROM A SWAMI OFFICIALLY. HENCE, I HAD TO ACCEPT THE ROBE FROM SWAMI ATMANANDA GIRI WHO WAS THEN THE OFFICIAL REPRESENTATIVE OF PARAMHANSA YOGANANDAJI. I WAS ALSO INFLUENCED IN IN MY DECISION BY MY FRIENDS AND OTHERS IN THE Y. S. S. TO FULFIL THE SILENT WISH OF PARAMAHANSA YOGANANDAJI AND TO RECEIVE THE ROBE FROM THE CHIEF SPIRITUAL DIRECTOR OF Y. S. S. INDIA . . ." (MY STRUGGLE FOR SELF-REALIZATION, AN AUTOBIOGRAPHY, P. 17)

Yogananda did not give 'sannyas' to Faye Wright; so after Yogananda's death she sought out Shankarcharya of Puri, His Holiness Jagadguru Sri Bharati Tirtha. He gave her entry into the swami order during his visit with Faye at SRF headquarters in 1958. As I understand the story His Holiness instructed Daya Mataji to correct

Yogananda's spiritual agnomen to paramahansa allegedly in accordance with Sanskrit and to show due reverence to Yogananda's spiritual stature.

What is intriguing to me is that Faye took this so much to heart that in 1958 she got the Board of Directors to approve adding the extra letter into Yogananda's signature: from this

to this:

"Love is the song of the soul, singing to God."

In the signature below the arrows indicate where the extra 'a' comes from. It is Yogananda's handwriting, but comparison shows it is a copy of the first 'a' in Yogananda's 'Yogananda' Signature.

If you think this is impossible, check out another photographic 'impossibility' by checking #16 in the Appendix Reference. There you will see one picture, twice. Once you see Swami Dhirananda, and then you don't . . . hmmmm.

In any other country this probably would be called forgery. But SRF, Inc. to this day puts it out as if Yogananda himself regularly honored himself with the extra 'a'. And, to make this point about SRF, Inc., pushing this narrative, I included the picture above with his signature underneath it: SRF, Inc., published it that way in the 1983 *Songs of the Soul* edition mentioned earlier. I believe USC's Josiah Royce would call this "an existential lie."

In this matter I give Sister Daya credit for her avowed love for God, and her loyalty to her '*sannyas*' guru, Sri Bharati Tirtha. Her love for God she beautifully describes in that tape recording of her 1948 death experience when Mother asked her "would you stay for me?" Faye wonderfully yields and adds, "Mother, all I have to offer is my love for you." And Faye reports that the Divine Mother responded, "that is all I ask."

During my visit with Daya Ma in 2012 she gave me wonderful and insightful guidance on finishing this life. Rajarsi, Gyanamataji, Mrinalini, Durga Ma, and others were with us in the same room. They concurred with her assessment.

Much as I needed (and cherish) the guidance from Divine Mother through Daya Ma, I am not blinded to my other realization (that was given without words) that Ma (and the others) acknowledge that this earth (including SRF, Inc.) is Divine Mother's play, and that She is the doer, neither Ma nor the others nor I. In other words no words of regret or commendation were ever considered or expressed in that meeting.

So rather than do a diatribe here about SRF, Inc.'s rationale for changing the spelling of Yogananda's name, I would rather raise a wonderful question, based on Daya Ma's loyalty to Sri Bharati Tirtha, her sannyas guru: how many gurus does one get?

Yogananda clearly teaches, not only in the Autobiography of a Yogi, but in these Praecepta, that a disciple has only one guru, "We can have many teachers first, but only one Guru, and no more teachers afterward." (Step IV, Praecepta 86)

Lahiri Mahasaya did not require disciples to give up their family guru or change outward family and social norms. Swami Satyananda says,

LAHIRI MAHASAYA HAD NO DESIRE TO FORM ANY GROUPS, AND AS SUCH, HE DID NOT ASK HIS DISCIPLES TO CHANGE THEIR SOCIETAL NORMS, DAILY DUTIES, PERFORMANCE OF WORSHIP OR RITUAL, OR THE INDIVIDUAL'S PERSONAL FEELINGS FOR GOD. HE WOULD ADVISE THEM TO PRACTICE WITH RESPECT AND TRUTHFULNESS, AND THROUGH KRIYAYOGA SADHANA ALONE, THE KNOWLEDGE THAT REVEALED ITSELF AND THE GOD-INTOXICATION THAT MANIFESTED, WOULD HE ATTRACT THE DISCIPLES' SIGHTS THAT DIRECTION. (YOGA NIKETAN. A COLLECTION OF BIOGRAPHIES OF 4 KRIYA YOGA GURUS (KINDLE LOCATIONS 467-470). YOGA NIKETAN, INC.. KINDLE EDITION.)

While persistently and lovingly referring to Sriyukteswar as his guru, there are times when Yogananda called him his 'proxy-guru,' meaning the interim role Sriyukteswar played on behalf of Babaji to prepare Yogananda for his spiritual role.

Even in Praeceptum 18 (p. 2) Yogananda unabashedly calls intuition the guru:

"THE CHRIST-LIKE GURU-PRECEPTOR, INTUITION, MUST COME WITH THE WHIP OF SELF CONTROL TO DRIVE AWAY THE MATERIALLY BUSY, RESTLESS THOUGHTS, AND MAKE THE TEMPLE OF SILENCE INTO A TEMPLE OF GOD."

It is only in reading the works of Yogananda's Indian disciples (such as Bidyananda and Sachidananda) or those of his childhood friend Satyananda (who ran the Ranchi School) that reference is made to 'sannyas guru.'

For   twenty years Swami Bidyanandaji continued in the YSS work after Yogananda initiated him in 1936 into discipleship (and Kriya). He tells the story of how he met his *sannyas* guru through Daya Mata.

"IN OCTOBER, 1958, SRI DAYA MATA, PRESIDENT OF THE SELF REALISATION FELLOWSHIP (THE MAIN ORGANISATION OF YOGODA SATSANGA) VISITED INDIA FROM AMERICA. . . . SHE SUMMONED ME TO MEET HER . . . THE MOMENT WE MET, SHE FIRST ENQUIRED WHY TILL THEN I WAS NOT INITIATED IN MONKHOOD (SANNYAS). DAYA WAS A CO-DISCIPLE SISTER FULL OF COMPASSION IN HER BODY AND MIND AND A NOBLE SOUL. I REPLIED FORCEFULLY, "WHO IS THE SAINT IN OUR INSTITUTION HAVING THE PROPER AUTHORITY TO ADMINISTER MONKHOOD INITIATION OR SANNYAS? . . ." DAYAMATA BECAME THOUGHTFUL, AFFECTIONATELY PATTED MY BACK AND REMAINED SILENT. . . THE SUBJECT OF MONKHOOD WAS NO MORE DISCUSSED.

". . . THEN ONE DAY I RECEIVED A LETTER FROM DAYAMATA. SHE . . . HAD TALKED WITH THE SHANKARACHARYA SRI KRISHNA TIRTHA BHARATI OF PURI GOBARDHAN MATH AND ARRANGED FOR MY INITIATION IN THE MONASTIC ORDER ALONG WITH BRAHMACHARI RAVI NARAYAN MAHARAJ OF PURI YOGODA ASHRAM. SHE WANTED TO KNOW IF I WAS AGREEABLE TO BE INITIATED BY THE SHANKARACHARYA. WHO WAS GOING TO LOSE THE RARE OPPORTUNITY OF INITIATION FROM THE SHANKARACHARYA HIMSELF? I IMMEDIATELY CONSENTED . . .HE DECIDED TO FORMALLY INITIATE MYSELF AND SRI RAVI NARAYAN AS MONKS ON 27TH MAY, 1959 AT OUR PURI ASHRAM.

". . . RAVI NARAYANJI AND MYSELF WERE GIVEN THE MONASTIC NAMES OF SWAMI HARIHARANANDA GIRI AND SWAMI BIDYANANDA GIRI RESPECTIVELY. . . THE KIND-HEARTED, GOD-MAN SHANKARACHARYAJI, AS A REPRESENTATIVE OF OUR DEPARTED GURU PARAMHANSA YOGANANDA, MADE US MONKS TO ENGAGE OURSELVES IN SELFLESS SERVICE FOR THE WELFARE OF ALL. (PP. 86-89 AD PASSIM, JEEVANSMRITI)"

An interesting feature of Swami Bidyanandaji's story is that at times of spiritual uncertainty he consulted his *sannyas* guru, whom he called the 'God-man' Shankaracharyaji in person for guidance. And at the same time Swamiji lovingly refers to Guru Yogananda as *Sriguru* and appropriately waited on his departed guru to make clear his will on various issues.

With respect notice the spelling of Yogananda's agnomen by Bidyanandaji.

I'll deal more with this issue of spelling in the chapter on "Church Doctrine and Defamation of Yogananda's Disciples."

How many gurus does a devotee need?: as many as are needed. Even Yogananda taught through stories that ultimately not only is 'God the guru' but at the highest level of spiritual development you and I are our own guru. If this seems too facile an explanation then read further in the chapter "God or Hitler and Mussolini." Likewise in the chapter on Yogananda's rationale for coming to America additional information will be given that continues to clarify this issue of one guru vs several.

Chapter 6. God or Hitler and Mussolini

There is a most amazing 1928 Christmas message to all nations from Yogananda in the East-West magazine; did he realize what history would be when he endorsed the uplifting guidance of Hitler:

"HITLER IS TO BE ADMIRED FOR LEAVING THE LEAGUE OF NATIONS BECAUSE PEACE CAN NEVER BE ATTAINED BY THE VICTOR AND VANQUISHED ATTITUDE, BUT ONLY ON A BASIS OF EQUALITY AND BROTHERHOOD. INSTEAD OF PREVENTING HITLER FROM HAVING EQUAL ARMAMENT WITH OTHER NATIONS, THE OTHER NATIONS SHOULD REDUCE ARMAMENTS TO THE LEVEL OF GERMANY, THEN THE MILLIONS OF DOLLARS THAT ARE THROWN AWAY ON IDLE BATTLESHIPS COULD BE USED FOR NATIONAL OR INTERNATIONAL PROSPERITY. AMERICA, FRANCE, AND GREAT BRITAIN SHOULD REDUCE THEIR ARMAMENTS FIRST, AND THEREBY DESTROY THE DESIRE OF JAPAN, RUSSIA, AND GERMANY TO BECOME EQUALLY ARMED. AN INSULTED, SNUBBED GERMANY, IF IT GETS AWAY FROM THE UPLIFTING GUIDANCE OF HITLER, MAY JOIN RUSSIA AND MAKE HER A MORE POWERFUL ENEMY OF FRANCE, AND SO ON. THE ALLIES MUST REDUCE THEIR OWN ARMAMENTS FIRST, AND THEN THEY WILL FIND OUT THAT EXAMPLE SPEAKS LOUDER THAN WORDS." (EAST-WEST MAGAZINE, DECEMBER, 1933, PAGE TWENTY-FIVE)

Perhaps Divine Mother was deliberately deceiving her son, Yogananda. As she says in the Bhagavad-Gita,"

"THE VEIL CAST BY MAYA, HOWEVER, IS HEAVY. EVEN MASTERS MUST MAKE A CONSCIOUS EFFORT TO CAST OFF ITS LAST LINGERING TRACES IN THEIR CONSCIOUSNESS." (PARAMHANSA YOGANANDA. THE ESSENCE OF THE BHAGAVAD GITA, 2ND EDITION: EXPLAINED BY PARAMHANSA YOGANANDA, AS REMEMBERED BY HIS DISCIPLE, SWAMI KRIYANANDA (KINDLE LOCATIONS 4130-4131). KINDLE EDITION.)

Yogananda seemed to admire Mussolini's mind, publishing a 1927 public speech,

"BENITO MUSSOLINI ON SCIENCE AND RELIGION
"THERE IS NO DOUBT THAT SCIENCE YEARNS TO ARRIVE AT THE FINAL REASON OF ALL THINGS. AFTER HAVING EXAMINED PHENOMENA, IT SEEKS TO EXPLAIN THEIR REASON.
"IT IS MY MODEST OPINION THAT SCIENCE WILL NEVER ARRIVE AT EXPLAINING THE WHEREFORE OF PHENOMENA, WHICH WILL ALWAYS REMAIN A ZONE OF MYSTERY, A CLOSED WALL.
"UPON THIS CLOSED WALL THE HUMAN SPIRIT MUST WRITE THE ONE WORD "GOD."
"THEREFORE, TO MY BELIEF, THERE IS NO QUESTION OF ANY CONFLICT BETWEEN SCIENCE AND FAITH. THESE MATTERS BELONG TO THE POLEMICS OF TWENTY OR THIRTY YEARS AGO, BUT I THINK THAT WE OF THIS GENERATION HAVE GONE BEYOND THIS POINT. SCIENCE HAS ITS OWN FIELD; THAT OF EXPERIENCE; RELIGION LIES ANOTHER FIELD, THAT OF THE SPIRIT.
"IT HAS BEEN SAID: WHAT IS THE USE OF ALL THE PHILOSOPHY OF THIS WORLD IF IT CANNOT TEACH US TO BEAR A TROUBLE WITH EQUANIMITY? THERE IS AN INTERMEDIATE ZONE SET APART FOR MEDITATION ON, RATHER THAN FOR EXAMINATION OF, THE SUPREME ENDS OF EXISTENCE.
"PHILOSOPHY ALONE CAN ILLUMINE SCIENCE AND BRING IT WITHIN THE REALM OF THE UNIVERSAL IDEA." (EAST-WEST MAGAZINE, VOL. II, NO. 4, MAY-JUNE)

Some years later Yogananda gave additional time to Mussolini, publishing in April, 1934, the following assessment of the 'master brain' of Mussolini.

"QUESTION: WHAT MESSAGE HAS HINDU PHILOSOPHY TO OFFER TOWARD SOLVING PRESENT-DAY PROBLEMS OF PEACE BETWEEN NATIONS AND AVERTING INTERNATIONAL DISASTERS?

"ANSWER: MAHATMA GANDHI IS THE WALKING PHILOSOPHER OF INDIA. HE HAS DEMONSTRATED THE PHILOSOPHY OF NONVIOLENCE AND NON-CO-OPERATION WITH EVIL SYSTEMS AND OF RESISTANCE BY A SPIRITUAL FORCE ONLY, IN THE FACE OF MACHINE GUNS, AND HAS THUS WON MORE SELF-GOVERNING PRIVILEGES FOR INDIA WITHIN A FEW YEARS THAN IRELAND ACCOMPLISHED IN 750 YEARS OF ARMED RESISTANCE.

"QUESTION: INDIVIDUALISM AND SOCIALISM ARE CONFLICTING PHILOSOPHIES IN THE MODERN WORLD. WHICH IS MORE LIKELY TO PREVAIL IN THE FUTURE?

"ANSWER: INDIVIDUAL PERFECTION AND SOCIAL UPLIFTMENT ARE INTERDEPENDENT. A MASTER BRAIN LIKE THAT OF MUSSOLINI DOES MORE GOOD THAN MILLIONS OF SOCIAL ORGANIZATIONS OF GROUP INTELLIGENCE. YET, IF MANY PERSONS IN A GROUP SHOULD DEVELOP THE BRAIN POWER OF A MUSSOLINI, THEY WOULD BE GREATER THAN THE INDIVIDUAL MUSSOLINI. GREAT INDIVIDUALS ARE SENT ON EARTH AS A PATTERN AFTER WHICH ORDINARY MEMBERS OF SOCIETY MUST MODEL THEMSELVES.

"QUESTION: DOES THE RISE, IN RECENT YEARS, OF DICTATORSHIPS AS FORMS OF GOVERNMENT INDICATE THE FAILURE AND ULTIMATE DOOM OF DEMOCRACY?

"ANSWER: A SOCIETY OF MORONS AND UNTHINKING PEOPLE WILL NEVER ESTABLISH A REAL DEMOCRACY. THE AVERAGE MAN CANNOT THINK CLEARLY, BUT IS RULED BY EXPLOSIONS OF HIS EMOTIONS. HE NEEDS THE MASTER MIND OF A DICTATOR IN ORDER TO THINK RIGHT AND DO RIGHT. WHEN THE MASS OF THE PEOPLE IN A NATION ARE QUALITATIVELY AND UNIFORMLY EDUCATED, THEY WILL FORM THE DEMOCRACY OF UNIVERSAL WISDOM AND AGREEMENT, AND WILL THEN BE ABLE TO GOVERN THEMSELVES SPONTANEOUSLY BY THE UNIVERSAL LAWS OF TRUTH. THEN DICTATORS WILL BE UNNECESSARY.

"ONE REAL WISE DICTATOR, LIKE PRESIDENT ROOSEVELT, IS MUCH BETTER THAN TOO MANY COOKS OF SMALL DICTATORS AND POLITICIANS, WHO SPOIL THE BROTH. MUCH IS DISCUSSED AND NOTHING ACCOMPLISHED WITH MANY. A WHOLE-HEARTED CO-OPERATION WITH THE NRA, AND WITH ACTIVE, WISE PRESIDENT ROOSEVELT, WILL BRING PROSPERITY AND INTERNATIONAL BALANCE." (AN INTERVIEW, BY SWAMI YOGANANDA, EAST-WEST MAGAZINE, FEBRUARY, 1934)

Previously Yogananda says to "Learn to understand the law of order which governs our actions." He seems to hold that that involves unselfish service to others, and that therein may be understood our roles and God's role.

In this Step (IV), Praeceptum 86 (p. 3) Yogananda points out what a true guru is:

"A SCRIPTURE, NO MATTER WHAT RECORDS OF SPIRITUAL TRUTHS IT CONTAINS, IS NOT AS USEFUL AS A SAINT, WHO IS VERITABLY A WALKING, TALKING, AND LIVING SCRIPTURE."

So we're looking then at the issues of the nature of the saint (or guru) and God as the only doer.

I am reminded of Arjuna's reaction after he had been granted the Vision of Vision by his guru. The scribe Saint Vyasa exquisitely 'words out' in literarily exquisite detail all the good, bad, and ugly that 'God' does in the name of this entertainment. And, to be clear, it's all 'God.' A pantheistic monotheism for real. And Arjuna, having his desire fulfilled (somewhat like Ramakrishna's Mathur mentioned earlier) says, "BELOVED LORD, LET ME SEE YOU AGAIN IN THE FORM FAMILIAR TO ME."

And the Krishna accommodates him.

Do you remember Christ Jesus' remark:

"THINK NOT THAT I AM COME TO SEND PEACE ON EARTH: I CAME NOT TO SEND PEACE, BUT A SWORD. FOR I AM COME TO SET A MAN AT VARIANCE AGAINST HIS FATHER, AND THE DAUGHTER AGAINST HER MOTHER, AND THE DAUGHTER IN LAW AGAINST HER MOTHER IN LAW." (MATTHEW 10:34, 35)

And yet Charles Wesley's song describes implores 'gentle Jesus, meek and mild"!

BUT TAKE ANOTHER LOOK AT THE BHAGAVAD-GITA ON THIS MATTER. ARJUNA'S COSMIC VISION IS STILL OF THE REALITY ON "THIS SIDE THE JORDAN."

"GAZE, THEN, THOU SON OF PRITHA! I MANIFEST FOR THEE THOSE HUNDRED THOUSAND THOUSAND SHAPES THAT CLOTHE MY MYSTERY: I SHOW THEE ALL MY SEMBLANCES, INFINITE, RICH, DIVINE, MY CHANGEFUL HUES, MY COUNTLESS FORMS. SEE! IN THIS FACE OF MINE, ADITYAS, VASUS, RUDRAS, ASWINS, AND MARUTS; SEE WONDERS UNNUMBERED, INDIAN PRINCE! REVEALED TO NONE SAVE THEE. BEHOLD! THIS IS THE UNIVERSE! -- LOOK! WHAT IS LIVE AND DEAD I GATHER ALL IN ONE -- IN ME! GAZE, AS THY LIPS HAVE SAID, ON GOD ETERNAL, VERY GOD! SEE ME! SEE WHAT THOU PRAYEST! THOU CANST NOT! -- NOR, WITH HUMAN EYES, ARJUNA! EVER MAYEST! THEREFORE I GIVE THEE SENSE DIVINE. HAVE OTHER EYES, NEW LIGHT! AND, LOOK! THIS IS MY GLORY, UNVEILED TO MORTAL SIGHT!" (ANONYMOUS. BHAGAVAD-GITA OR, THE SONG CELESTIAL (FROM THE MAHABHARATA) (MOBI) (PENGUIN CLASSICS) (KINDLE LOCATIONS 512-517). MOBILEREFERENCE. KINDLE EDITION.)

He hasn't yet entered into the Silence or as the Christians say, "the terrible day of the Lord."

Krishna reappears to Arjuna in his comforting form, but Krishna speaks of those who are

"MINE OWN, THE TRUE OF HEART, THE FAITHFUL -- STAYED ON ME, TAKING ME AS THEIR UTMOST BLESSEDNESS, THEY ARE NOT "MINE," BUT I -- EVEN I MYSELF!" (ANONYMOUS. BHAGAVAD-GITA OR, THE SONG CELESTIAL (FROM THE MAHABHARATA) (MOBI) (PENGUIN CLASSICS) (KINDLE LOCATIONS 371-372). MOBILEREFERENCE. KINDLE EDITION.)

So God, Hitler, or Mussolini becomes, ultimately, the Divine Doer alone says,

"ISAIAH 45:5 I AM THE LORD, AND THERE IS NONE ELSE, THERE IS NO GOD BESIDE ME: I GIRDED THEE, THOUGH THOU HAST NOT KNOWN ME: 6 THAT THEY MAY KNOW FROM THE RISING OF THE SUN, AND FROM THE WEST, THAT THERE IS NONE BESIDE ME. I AM THE LORD, AND THERE IS NONE ELSE. 7 I FORM THE LIGHT, AND CREATE DARKNESS: I MAKE PEACE, AND CREATE EVIL: I THE LORD DO ALL THESE THINGS. (MOBILEREFERENCE. THE HOLY BIBLE (KING JAMES VERSION, KJV) FOR KINDLE: THE OLD & NEW TESTAMENTS, DEUTEROCANONICAL LITERATURE, GLOSSARY & SUGGESTED READING LIST. ILLUSTRATED BY GUSTAVE DORE (MOBI SPIRITUAL) (KINDLE LOCATIONS 19763-19766). MOBILEREFERENCE. KINDLE EDITION.)

"I FORM THE LIGHT, AND CREATE DARKNESS: I MAKE PEACE, AND CREATE EVIL. I THE LORD DO ALL THESE THINGS." (IS 45:7)

Chapter 7. God as the Only Doer

The discussion "God or Hitler or Mussolini" sets up the understanding for the apparent sexual misbehavior of Yogananda, the original cause of my suicide so long ago.

Chris Isherwood tells a wonderful story about God as the only doer.

"MATHUR WAS A DISCIPLE OF RAMAKRISHNA. THE EXCERPT CLOSELY MODELS PSALM 37:23: "THE STEPS OF A RIGHTEOUS MAN ARE ORDERED BY THE LORD." MATHUR USED TO BEG RAMAKRISHNA TO COMMUNICATE ECSTASY TO HIM BY A TOUCH. RAMAKRISHNA TRIED TO DISSUADE HIM FROM THIS DESIRE, TELLING HIM HE WOULD DO MUCH BETTER TO WAIT AND BE PATIENT, AND THAT, ANYHOW, HE SHOULD KEEP HIS LIFE BALANCED BETWEEN DEVOTION TO GOD AND WORLDLY OBLIGATIONS; THAT BEING HIS DHARMA. BUT MATHUR PERSISTED, UNTIL RAMAKRISHNA SAID, `VERY WELL, I'LL ASK MOTHER ABOUT IT; SHE WILL DO AS SHE THINKS BEST.' A FEW DAYS LATER, MATHUR WENT INTO THE LOWER FORM OF SAMADHI AT HIS HOUSE IN CALCUTTA. THIS IS HOW RAMAKRISHNA WOULD DESCRIBE WHAT HAPPENED NEXT. 'HE SENT FOR ME; AND WHEN I WENT THERE I FOUND HIM ALTOGETHER CHANGED - HE WASN'T THE SAME MAN. WHENEVER HE SPOKE OF GOD, HE SHED FLOODS OF TEARS; HIS EYES WERE RED FROM WEEPING. AND HIS HEART WAS POUNDING. WHEN HE SAW ME, HE FELL DOWN AND CLASPED MY FEET. "FATHER," HE SAID, "I ADMIT IT - I'M BEATEN! I'VE BEEN IN THIS STATE FOR THE PAST THREE DAYS. I CAN'T APPLY MY MIND TO WORLDLY AFFAIRS, HOWEVER HARD I TRY. EVERYTHING IS GOING WRONG. PLEASE TAKE BACK THE ECSTASY YOU GAVE ME. I DON'T WANT IT." "BUT YOU BEGGED ME FOR ECSTASY," I SAID. "I KNOW I DID. AND IT IS INDEED A BLISSFUL STATE - BUT WHAT'S THE USE OF BLISS, WHEN ALL MY WORLDLY AFFAIRS ARE GOING TO PIECES? THIS ECSTASY OF YOURS, FATHER, IT ONLY SUITS YOU. THE REST OF US DON'T REALLY WANT IT. PLEASE TAKE IT BACK!"

"THEN I LAUGHED AND SAID, "THAT'S WHAT I TOLD YOU, ALL ALONG." "I KNOW YOU DID, FATHER. BUT WHAT I DIDN'T UNDERSTAND WAS THAT THIS THING LIKE A SPIRIT WOULD POSSESS ME, AND THAT I'D HAVE TO TAKE EVERY STEP AND DO EVERYTHING EXACTLY AS IT TOLD ME TO, TWENTY-FOUR HOURS A DAY!" SO THEN I JUST RUBBED MATHUR'S CHEST WITH MY HAND, AND HE WAS HIMSELF AGAIN.'" (CHRISTOPHER ISHERWOOD. RAMAKRISHNA AND HIS DISCIPLES (KINDLE LOCATION 1788-1798). KINDLE EDITION))

Yogananda used to talk of the "shock" of omnipresence and encourage disciples to use the Kriya technique to prepare the body for such purification.

"A MASTER BESTOWS THE DIVINE EXPERIENCE OF COSMIC CONSCIOUSNESS WHEN HIS DISCIPLE, BY MEDITATION, HAS STRENGTHENED HIS MIND TO A DEGREE WHERE THE VAST VISTAS WOULD NOT OVERWHELM HIM. THE EXPERIENCE CAN NEVER BE GIVEN THROUGH ONE'S MERE INTELLECTUAL WILLINGNESS OR OPEN-MINDEDNESS. ONLY ADEQUATE ENLARGEMENT BY YOGA PRACTICE AND DEVOTIONAL BHAKTI CAN PREPARE THE MIND TO ABSORB THE LIBERATING SHOCK OF OMNIPRESENCE. IT COMES WITH A NATURAL INEVITABILITY TO THE SINCERE DEVOTEE. HIS INTENSE CRAVING BEGINS TO PULL AT GOD WITH AN IRRESISTIBLE FORCE. THE LORD, AS THE COSMIC VISION, IS DRAWN BY THE SEEKER'S MAGNETIC ARDOR INTO HIS RANGE OF CONSCIOUSNESS." (Yogananda, Paramhansa.

Autobiography of a Yogi (Reprint of Original 1946 Edition) (p. 95). Crystal Clarity Publishers - A. Kindle Edition.))

"THE EXPERIENCE CAN NEVER BE GIVEN THROUGH ONE'S MERE INTELLECTUAL WILLINGNESS OR OPEN-MINDEDNESS," HE POINTS OUT. AT LEAST ONE OF THE CHARGES LEVELLED AGAINST YOGANANDA IN THE 1928 MIAMI SCANDAL WAS THAT "THE SON OF ANOTHER WOMAN REPORTED THAT HE HAD FOUND HIS MOTHER TRYING TO WALK ON THE MIAMI RIVER BECAUSE "YOGANANDA TOLD HER SHE COULD DO IT."" (New York Times, Feb. 4, 1928)

Of course Yogananda didn't tell her she could do it, and a timely telegram "from James McLachian, former United States District Attorney at Los Angeles and former member of Congress from California, stating that he had known Yogananda intimately for four years and that he was one of the most godly men he ever knew," was sent to Yogananda's attorneys and "was exhibited by attorneys." (Ibid) (See the NYTimes article in the Appendix References, #1)

It should be pointed out that McLachian was actually the comptroller of the Mother Center property, since Yogananda could not, as an alien, own property in the State of California.

In the chapter on American Identity I recounted Yogananda's his visit Ananda Moy Ma. She told how her husband was shocked by the spiritual (rather than lustful) current emanating from her physical body.

Rajarsi Janakananda touched his Master's wrist during a Christmas meditation, and immediately fell unconscious to the floor.

In a later discussion of his motive James Lynn explained that he wanted to see the same Christ that Yogananda was seeing.

There is a most amazing 1928 Christmas message to all nations from Yogananda in the East-West magazine; did he realize what history would be when he endorsed the uplifting guidance of Hitler. See the chapter "God or Hitler and Mussolini" for further discussion.

Throughout the Bhagavad-Gita the Lord emphasizes that all is wrought in this cosmos through Lord, even those who cling to the skirts of religion.

"THERE BE THOSE, TOO, WHOSE KNOWLEDGE, TURNED ASIDE BY THIS DESIRE OR THAT, GIVES THEM TO SERVE SOME LOWER GODS, WITH VARIOUS RITES, CONSTRAINED BY THAT WHICH MOULDETH THEM. UNTO ALL SUCH -- WORSHIP WHAT SHRINE THEY WILL, WHAT SHAPES, IN FAITH --. 'TIS I WHO GIVE THEM FAITH! I AM CONTENT! THE HEART THUS ASKING FAVOUR FROM ITS GOD, DARKENED BUT ARDENT, HATH THE END IT CRAVES, THE LESSER BLESSING -- BUT 'TIS I WHO GIVE! YET SOON IS WITHERED WHAT SMALL FRUIT THEY REAP: THOSE MEN OF LITTLE MINDS, WHO WORSHIP SO, GO WHERE THEY WORSHIP, PASSING WITH THEIR GODS. BUT MINE COME UNTO ME! BLIND ARE THE EYES WHICH DEEM TH' UNMANIFESTED MANIFEST, NOT COMPREHENDING ME IN MY TRUE SELF! IMPERISHABLE, VIEWLESS, UNDECLARED, HIDDEN BEHIND MY MAGIC VEIL OF SHOWS, I AM NOT SEEN BY ALL; I AM NOT KNOWN -- UNBORN AND CHANGELESS -- TO THE IDLE WORLD. BUT I, ARJUNA! KNOW ALL THINGS WHICH WERE, AND ALL WHICH ARE, AND ALL WHICH ARE TO BE, ALBEIT NOT ONE AMONG THEM KNOWETH ME!" (Anonymous. Bhagavad-Gita or, The Song Celestial (From the Mahabharata) (mobi) (Penguin Classics) (Kindle Locations 373-380). MobileReference. Kindle Edition.)

"'Tis I who give them faith! I am content!" Isn't that beautiful!

Then Krishna says that Arjuna will fight, willingly or unwillingly, because:

"THERE LIVES A MASTER IN THE HEARTS OF MEN MAKETH THEIR DEEDS, BY SUBTLE PULLING -- STRINGS, DANCE TO WHAT TUNE HE WILL.

"SO KRISHNA SAYS TO FIGHT WILLINGLY GIVING THE RESULTS INTO GOD'S HANDS:

"WITH ALL THY SOUL TRUST HIM, AND TAKE HIM FOR THY SUCCOUR, PRINCE! SO -- ONLY SO, ARJUNA! -- SHALT THOU GAIN -- BY GRACE OF HIM -- THE UTTERMOST REPOSE, THE ETERNAL PLACE!" (ANONYMOUS. BHAGAVAD-GITA OR, THE SONG CELESTIAL (FROM THE MAHABHARATA) (MOBI) (PENGUIN CLASSICS) (KINDLE LOCATIONS 857-859). MOBILEREFERENCE. KINDLE EDITION.)

This final word is in final chapter 18, after Arjuna has been given the Kriya key (Chapter 4) and the Cosmic Vision (Chapter 11).

"NAY! BUT ONCE MORE TAKE MY LAST WORD, MY UTMOST MEANING HAVE! PRECIOUS THOU ART TO ME; RIGHT WELL-BELOVED! LISTEN! I TELL THEE FOR THY COMFORT THIS. GIVE ME THY HEART! ADORE ME! SERVE ME! CLING IN FAITH AND LOVE AND REVERENCE TO ME! SO SHALT THOU COME TO ME! I PROMISE TRUE, FOR THOU ART SWEET TO ME! AND LET GO THOSE -- RITES AND WRIT DUTIES! FLY TO ME ALONE! MAKE ME THY SINGLE REFUGE! I WILL FREE THY SOUL FROM ALL ITS SINS! BE OF GOOD CHEER!" (ANONYMOUS. BHAGAVAD-GITA OR, THE SONG CELESTIAL (FROM THE MAHABHARATA) (MOBI) (PENGUIN CLASSICS) (KINDLE LOCATIONS 860-863). MOBILEREFERENCE. KINDLE EDITION.)

And once more: "And let go those -- Rites and writ duties!"

Here the Lord takes everything away from anything man may conceptualize, religionize, weaponize, ritualize, and says, "Make me thy single refuge!" and then "Be of good cheer!"

This so reminds me of all the Jewish prophetic and poetic writings "I will keep him in perfect peace" and "be still and know" although I note that in none of those is a technique given for attaining perfect peace or stillness.

Yet it is the Lord alone; and here lies understanding: if one thinks that God is Jadava Krishna or Jesus Christ, or that Jadava is speaking here or that Jesus is saying, "I am the way, the truth and the life," then one is worshipping, as the Lord says above, "lesser gods."

"UNTO ALL SUCH -- WORSHIP WHAT SHRINE THEY WILL, WHAT SHAPES, IN FAITH --. 'TIS I WHO GIVE THEM FAITH! I AM CONTENT! THE HEART THUS ASKING FAVOUR FROM ITS GOD, DARKENED BUT ARDENT, HATH THE END IT CRAVES, THE LESSER BLESSING -- BUT 'TIS I WHO GIVE!"

Krishna gives the clue:

". . . BUT MINE OWN, THE TRUE OF HEART, THE FAITHFUL -- STAYED ON ME, TAKING ME AS THEIR UTMOST BLESSEDNESS, THEY ARE   NOT "MINE," BUT I -- EVEN I MYSELF!" (ANONYMOUS. BHAGAVAD-GITA OR, THE SONG CELESTIAL (FROM THE MAHABHARATA) (MOBI) (PENGUIN CLASSICS) (KINDLE LOCATIONS 371-372). MOBILEREFERENCE. KINDLE EDITION.)

Here then is the Divine as 'all in all.' Those who go through the purification know who they are, the rest of us still struggle in the dark...but the Divine is the Doer, "in whom we live and move and have our being."

Chapter 8. Rationale for Yogananda's American Work

Spiritualizing America

Yogananda ostensibly gives his rationale for coming to America in Autobiography of a Yogi, chapter 37, i.e., God has called him to go:

"AMERICA! SURELY THESE PEOPLE ARE AMERICANS!" THIS WAS MY THOUGHT AS A PANORAMIC VISION OF WESTERN FACES PASSED BEFORE MY INWARD VIEW.

"IMMERSED IN MEDITATION, I WAS SITTING BEHIND SOME DUSTY BOXES IN THE STOREROOM OF THE RANCHI SCHOOL. A PRIVATE SPOT WAS DIFFICULT TO FIND DURING THOSE BUSY YEARS WITH THE YOUNGSTERS!

"THE VISION CONTINUED; A VAST MULTITUDE, GAZING AT ME INTENTLY, SWEPT ACTORLIKE ACROSS THE STAGE OF CONSCIOUSNESS.

"THE STOREROOM DOOR OPENED; AS USUAL, ONE OF THE YOUNG LADS HAD DISCOVERED MY HIDING PLACE. "COME HERE, BIMAL," I CRIED GAILY. "I HAVE NEWS FOR YOU: THE LORD IS CALLING ME TO AMERICA!"

"TO AMERICA?" THE BOY ECHOED MY WORDS IN A TONE THAT IMPLIED I HAD SAID "TO THE MOON."

"YES! I AM GOING FORTH TO DISCOVER AMERICA, LIKE COLUMBUS. HE THOUGHT HE HAD FOUND INDIA; SURELY THERE IS A KARMIC LINK BETWEEN THOSE TWO LANDS!"

"BIMAL SCAMPERED AWAY; SOON THE WHOLE SCHOOL WAS INFORMED BY THE TWO-LEGGED NEWSPAPER, I SUMMONED THE BEWILDERED FACULTY AND GAVE THE SCHOOL INTO ITS CHARGE.

"I KNOW YOU WILL KEEP LAHIRI MAHASAYA'S YOGA IDEALS OF EDUCATION EVER TO THE FORE," I SAID. "I SHALL WRITE YOU FREQUENTLY; GOD WILLING, SOMEDAY I SHALL BE BACK."

"TEARS STOOD IN MY EYES AS I CAST A LAST LOOK AT THE LITTLE BOYS AND THE SUNNY ACRES OF RANCHI. A DEFINITE EPOCH IN MY LIFE HAD NOW CLOSED, I KNEW; HENCEFORTH I WOULD DWELL IN FAR LANDS. I ENTRAINED FOR CALCUTTA A FEW HOURS AFTER MY VISION.

"THE FOLLOWING DAY I RECEIVED AN INVITATION TO SERVE AS THE DELEGATE FROM INDIA TO AN INTERNATIONAL CONGRESS OF RELIGIOUS LIBERALS IN AMERICA. IT WAS TO CONVENE THAT YEAR IN BOSTON, UNDER THE AUSPICES OF THE AMERICAN UNITARIAN ASSOCIATION.

"MY HEAD IN A WHIRL, I SOUGHT OUT SRI YUKTESWAR IN SERAMPORE. "GURUJI, I HAVE JUST BEEN INVITED TO ADDRESS A RELIGIOUS CONGRESS IN AMERICA. SHALL I GO?"

""ALL DOORS ARE OPEN FOR YOU," MASTER REPLIED SIMPLY. "IT IS NOW OR NEVER.""
(YOGANANDA, PARAMHANSA. AUTOBIOGRAPHY OF A YOGI (REPRINT OF ORIGINAL 1946 EDITION, CH. 37, "I GO TO AMERICA," P. 219). CRYSTAL CLARITY PUBLISHERS - A. KINDLE EDITION.)

Through means quite miraculous within the next few weeks Yogananda's trip was secured, although the purpose is never quite clear. Later Yogananda would mention in private meetings with various groups of disciples that many of those present were in that vision of his disciples.

The Autobiography of a Yogi makes it sound like the trip is for purposes of spreading the 'creedless teachings of Kriya yoga.' His father is the voice: "I GIVE YOU THIS MONEY," HE SAID, "NOT IN MY CAPACITY AS A FATHER, BUT AS A FAITHFUL DISCIPLE OF LAHIRI MAHASAYA. GO THEN TO THAT FAR WESTERN LAND; SPREAD THERE THE CREEDLESS TEACHINGS OF KRIYA YOGA." (Ibid., p. 220. Crystal Clarity Publishers - A. Kindle Edition.)

After Yogananda's decision to go to America he relates this meeting with Babaji.

". . . BABAJI ADDRESSED ME AGAIN. "YOU ARE THE ONE I HAVE CHOSEN TO SPREAD THE MESSAGE OF KRIYA YOGA IN THE WEST. LONG AGO I MET YOUR GURU YUKTESWAR AT A KUMBHA MELA; I TOLD HIM THEN I WOULD SEND YOU TO HIM FOR TRAINING." (OP. CIT., LOC. CIT. CRYSTAL CLARITY PUBLISHERS - A. KINDLE EDITION.)

Interestingly though not contradictorily Sriyukteswar's first disciple (the householder Matilal Mukhopadhyaya [aka Mukerjee]) states that Yogananda went to America and initiated many Americans in Rajayoga. He mentions nothing of Kriya. (Atma Katha: The Authorized Story of Sriyukteswar's First Disciple: Second 2016 Reprint (Kindle Locations 677-685)). UNKNOWN. Kindle Edition.)

I mention this because the narrative would have you believe that Yogananda came to America without a single friend, and the rest is history . . . yet only three years into his American calling (i.e., by 1923) Yogananda writes to Dr. Lewis' wife that in his next incarnation he won't be saddled (my choice of words) with organizational responsibilities.

And nowhere prior to his departure to America is there discussion about starting an organization for spreading Kriya teachings. Certainly Lahiri had forbidden such.

And as romantic or intriguing as the narrative may seem about going all alone, it neither was that way nor did it have to be that way . . . Yogananda constantly admits in letters that he is no business man and has to learn America's business methods. By the time JJ Lynn came along Yogananda still apparently hadn't learned business methods, because he mistook the gift of cafeteria stock market shares that JJ Lynn had sent (which would have provided a consistent income for Yogananda's enterprise) and he sold them paying off the Mother Center mortgage and other debts.

A review of the letters of Brenda Lewis in her story of her parents' lives (*Treasures Against Time*) will provide ample documentation of these remarks (as will a review of Durga Ma's A Paramhansa Yogananda Trilogy of Divine Love).

After reading Sara Ann Levinsky's biography of Swami Paramananda, *A Bridge of Dreams*, one realizes that Yogananda landed in Boston 'smack dab' in the middle of a spiritual community that had been successfully converted to the Vedantic way of thinking through the 14 years of tireless efforts of Paramanandaji. He was an excellent resource and entry point for Yogananda into the societal and community leadership; yet Yogananda apparently lived alone without contacting him. Paramananda was prepared to support Yogananda in any manner needed; but Yogananda 'went it alone' (my choice of words). Even the future Sri Nerode was already in America (and at Harvard!) but Yogananda doesn't use him or even consult him. And in less than five years Yogananda's merchandising of his lectures across America caused Paramananda and other Hindu leaders to shake their heads in disgust at this method of advertising India's sweet unguent of solitary meditation.

"THE TACTICS AND PACE OF SUCH BRAINSTORMING MINISTRY DID NOT ATTRACT SWAMI PARAMANANDA. YET PARAMANANDAJI PAID A PRICE FOR YOGANANDA'S STYLE:
"HE NEVER CONDEMNED ANY FIGURE, BUT TO HIS COMMUNITY HE DISCLOSED HIS DISDAIN FOR "ANYONE WHO GOES AFTER SENSATIONALISM."
"DESPITE ALL DISAVOWALS, PARAMANANDA COULD NOT ESCAPE THE BACKLASH AGAINST OTHER HINDU TEACHERS. ONCE HE WAS SCHEDULED TO SPEAK IN LOUISVILLE IMMEDIATELY AFTER SWAMI YOGANANDA APPEARED IN THAT CITY. THE CHRISTIAN CLERGY'S PROTEST AGAINST YOGANANDA'S ADVERTISEMENT APPEARING ON THE CHURCH PAGE MADE THE NEWSPAPERS RELUCTANT EVEN TO ANNOUNCE SWAMI PARAMANANDA. HIS LECTURES HAD TO BE LISTED AS "REVEREND PARAMANANDA."
"EVEN GENUINE HINDU SPIRITUAL TEACHERS LIKE SWAMI YOGANANDA PROJECTED AN IMAGE OF HINDU SPIRITUALITY DIFFERENT FROM THE ONE WHICH PARAMANANDA FOR TWO DECADES HAD SOUGHT TO ESTABLISH IN AMERICA. USING MADISON AVENUE TECHNIQUES SUCH AS PROMOTIONAL LETTERS AND PROMINENT NEWSPAPER AND BILLBOARD ADVERTISEMENTS, YOGANANDA OFFERED, FOR $25, A THREE-PART CORRESPONDENCE COURSE ON SPIRITUAL TECHNIQUES. PARAMANANDA'S FOLLOWERS WERE SHOCKED TO SEE PICTURES OF SWAMI YOGANANDA SMILING DOWN ON THEM IN THE BOSTON TROLLEY. PARAMANANDA RESPONDED SOMETIMES BY BECOMING EVEN MORE LOW-KEY;

WHEN HE SAW SWAMI YOGANANDA'S LARGE ADVERTISEMENTS IN THE LOS ANGELES NEWSPAPERS, HE WITHDREW HIS NOTICES ENTIRELY." (A BRIDGE OF DREAMS, PP. 263-371, AD PASSIM)

Dhirananda's 1935 lawsuit against Yogananda for contracted money owed brought out similar descriptions of Yogananda's style adding that a $4,000 a year advance man (actually 'Captain' Rashid whom Yogananda had met aboard ship) would go to these cities for promotional purposes.

That these three swamis were well known in the American religious scene is shown in the news article by Los Angeles Times Religion Editor James M. Warnack, a close associate and supporter of Yogananda in the early days after the move to Los Angeles, "Who are the swamis?," (Los Angeles Times, Dec. 25, 1932).

"SINCE SWAMI VIVEKANANDA CAME TO THIS COUNTRY TO ATTEND THE FIRST WORLD'S FAIR AT CHICAGO NEARLY THIRTY YEARS AGO, MORE SWAMIS FROM INDIA HAVE VISITED THE UNITED STATES THAN IN ALL OTHER PERIODS OF AMERICAN HISTORY AND TODAY THERE ARE MORE SWAMIS TO THE SQUARE MILE IN SOUTHERN CALIFORNIA THAN IN ANY OTHER SECTION OF THE COUNTRY. . . WITHIN THE LAST TWO DECADES MANY OF THESE SWAMIS HAVE VISITED LOS ANGELES FOR THE PURPOSE OF TEACHING THE RELIGION WHICH THEY PROFESS, AND SEVERAL OF THEM ARE HERE TODAY. BEST KNOWN IN THE SOUTHLAND TODAY ARE YOGANANDA, DHIRANANDA AND PARAMANANDA."

Warnack goes on to enunciate one of the principles which guided me to quit SRF, Inc. after forty years membership in that august organization.

". . . UNDOUBTEDLY THERE IS A GULF BETWEEN HINDUISM AND ORTHODOX CHRISTIANITY WHICH CANNOT BE BRIDGED. FOR INSTANCE, WHILE THE HINDU ACCEPTS JESUS, THE CHRIST, AS A MEMBER OF HIS PANTHEON, AND REGARDS HIM AS DIVINE, HE DOES NOT ACCEPT HIM AS "THE ONLY BEGOTTEN," THE SOLE SON OF GOD, AND DOES NOT CONSIDER CHRIST AS THE WORLD'S ONLY SAVIOR."

To my knowledge Yogananda ignored this gulf, initially calling for a "Church of All Religions." But of course once he incorporated into SRF, Inc., he set his version of the self-realization movement on a sectarian and apparently downhill track. Just two years after incorporating Yogananda handwrites a letter (March, 1937) to Sri Nerode lamenting in Bengali "I HAVE EATEN S**T FOR THIS ORGANIZATION." (see p. 969 of Swami Satyeswaranandaji's book *Mahamuni Babaji and His Legacy*)

Warnack goes on to talk of Yogananda's followers.

"FROM A STANDPOINT OF PUBLIC INTEREST, THE MOST SPECTACULAR SWAMI IN LOS ANGELES IS SWAMI YOGANANDA, WHOSE HEADQUARTERS ARE AT MT. WASHINGTON CENTER, HIGHLAND PARK. THIS MAN, WITH HIS LONG, DARK HAIR AND MIDNIGHT EYES, NUMBERS HIS FOLLOWERS BY THE THOUSANDS. IN HIS LITTLE COLONY ON THE HILL ARE SCORES OF MEN AND WOMEN WHO SEEM DEVOTED TO HIM AND HIS DOCTRINES, AND HIS LECTURERS ON SUNDAY AFTERNOONS ATTRACT HUNDREDS OF PERSONS, SOME HUMBLE AND IGNORANT, OTHERS MERELY CURIOUS."

Perhaps Warnack is accurate in his assessment of Yogananda's status as "the most spectacular swami in Los Angeles."

Warnack's frequently published articles in Yogananda's East-West magazine and his support of Yogananda wain within a few more years when Yogananda forbids Virginia Wright from having a romantic interest in Warnack's son Jimmy.

The story is related in an interview with Srimati Nerode:

"JIMMY WARNOCK [SIC] ALWAYS FELT HIS FATHER OUT SHOWN HIM, BECAUSE HIS FATHER COULD TELL YOU JOKES FOR HOURS ON END. AT FIRST SHE [SRIMATI] PLAYED WITH JIMMY AND IT TOOK JIMMY A YEAR OR SO TO REALIZE THAT SHE WAS OLDER. SRIMATI WAS ONE OF NINE CHILDREN AND WAS USED TO PLAYING WITH HER BROTHERS. JIMMY WAS AN ONLY CHILD SO HE WAS LACKING IN COMPANIONSHIP AND WANTED TO PLAY. HE ORIGINALLY WOULD HAVE BEEN ABOUT 10 YEARS OLD, BUT WHEN HE WAS DATING VIRGINIA, HE WOULD HAVE BEEN ABOUT 17 OR SO.

"SHE SAID THAT SY [SWAMI YOGANANDA] WHEN HE FOUND OUT ABOUT VIRGINIA'S SEEING OF JIMMY, ABSOLUTELY FORBID IT. JIMMY AND VIRGINIA HAD SEEN EACH OTHER PERHAPS THREE TIMES OR SO. SY AND MRS. WRIGHT WATCHED VIRGINIA TO SEE THAT SHE DIDN'T TRY TO GO OUT WITH JIMMY. VIRGINIA JUST CRIED, SHE WAS HEARTBROKEN. SY ABSOLUTELY FORBID IT EVEN AT THE EXPENSE OF HIS LOSING JAMES WARNOCK [SIC] AS HIS FRIEND AND LOYAL SUPPORTER." (APPENDIX REFERENCE #20, INTERVIEW WITH MRS. NERODE)

Having a spectacular status in Los Angeles may not have been the best thing for Yogananda or his mission. Certainly the other two swamis offered God-realization but without the hyperbole.

Interestingly Swami Paramananda, the elder statesman of the three swamis, had far more experience with Americans, and though their paths in many ways were parallel, it was Paramanandaji's work that was paramount:

They both had 'Sister Dayas', Paramanandaji's went on to sainthood; they both had ashrams in Los Angeles, 1923 La Crescenta Ananda-Ashram for Paramanandaji, and 1925 'Mother Center' for Yoganandaji. They both withdrew from their organizations for a brief time: Paramanandaji in mid-1920's when the 'backbiting' at Ananda-Ashram caused him to have heart trouble, and Yogananda in 1929 when he felt betrayed by Dhiranandaji. Both of them had successful books that had been compiled by disciples from written notes and public speeches. Paramananda's *The Path of Devotion* became an instant classic in America before the 1920's. (Appendix Reference #23, for an early listing of Swamiji's books).

In Ms. Keyes' autobiography *Sundial: I Count the Sunny Hours*, one sees further into the different personalities and evangelistic styles of Yoganandaji and his Yogoda associate, Swami Dhiranandaji.

"I WAS MUCH MORE COMFORTABLE WITH YOGANANDA'S PARTNER, DHIRANANDA. HIS HAIR WAS CUT NEATLY. HE WORE AN ORANGE-COLORED MINISTERIAL ROBE WITH A PRIEST'S COLLAR. HE WAS MORE APPROACHABLE. ONE COULD TALK TO HIM ON ANY SUBJECT, SCIENCE, LITERATURE, ART — MANY THINGS BESIDES RELIGION.

"BOTH MEN HAD BEEN STUDENTS OF THE GREAT MASTER, SRI YUKTESWAR. THEY HAD TAUGHT IN A BOY'S SCHOOL IN INDIA. AFTER YOGANANDA HAD ESTABLISHED HIMSELF IN CALIFORNIA HE HAD INVITED DHIRANANDA TO FOLLOW HIM TO AMERICA. HOWEVER, TEACHING SMALL BOYS WHO WERE RELIGIOUSLY ORIENTED FROM THEIR FAMILY BACKGROUNDS WAS VERY DIFFERENT FROM APPEALING TO ADULT WESTERN AUDIENCES SO THAT THE WORK COULD BE FINANCIALLY SOLVENT.

"DHIRANANDA HAD A DEMANDING CURIOSITY AND INTENSE NATURE. HE WAS EAGER TO FIND WAYS TO PROVE THE ANCIENT TRUTHS. HE FELT AMERICANS FAVORED SCIENTIFIC PROOF RATHER THAN FOLLOWING THE TRADITIONAL GURU-CHELA RELATIONSHIP WITH DEVOTION.

"I LISTENED TO BOTH MEN   FOR MONTHS BUT WHEN I HAD A QUESTION, I WENT TO DHIRANANDA."

So the question for this chapter becomes, what was Yogananda trying to do, once he arrived in America?

The following excerpt is taken from "Spiritualizing America" (East-West magazine, July-August, 1927, p. 15; a copy of the original is #5 in the Appendix

Reference section of this book) and it quotes Yogananda's ideal of 'spiritualizing America' through modern merchandising means.

"THE FOLLOWING APPEARED IN THE DERRY, NEW HAMPSHIRE, NEWS FOR APRIL 29TH; UNDER THE HEADING, "DID YOU EVER STOP TO THINK? ":

"R. J. CROMIE, PUBLISHER OF THE VANCOUVER SUN, SAYS:

"THAT MASS EDUCATION IS, THRU THE NEWSPAPERS, DOING SOME WONDERFUL THINGS FOR THE NORTH AMERICAN CONTINENT.

"THAT SUBJECTS LIKE (A) PHYSICAL MECHANICS, (B) FOOD CHEMISTRY, (C) MENTAL MECHANICS, ARE THREE SUBJECTS WHICH LEND THEMSELVES TO NEWSPAPER PROMOTION IN A WAY WHICH WILL BE OF TREMENDOUS SERVICE TO THE MILLIONS OF NEWSPAPER READERS OF AMERICA,

"THAT THESE SUBJECTS CAN BE 'HENRY FORDED' AND MERCHANDISED TO THE MASSES IN JUST THE SAME WAY AS AN INDUSTRIAL PRODUCT IS MERCHANDISED.

"THAT ALONG THE LINE OF (A) PHYSICAL MECHANICS, BERNARR MACFADDEN, OF PHYSICAL CULTURE, HAS FOR TWENTY YEARS LED THE FIELD UNTIL TODAY THERE IS EVERYWHERE A CONSCIOUSNESS OF THE NECESSITY OF PHYSICAL WELL-BEING.

"THAT ALONG THE LINE OF (B) FOOD CHEMISTRY. DR. FRANK MCCOY OF LOS ANGELES IS PRE-EMINENT IN HIS CLASS.

"THAT IN (C) MENTAL MECHANICS. ARTHUR BRISBANE HAS FOR TWENTY YEARS LED THE FIELD. OTHERS LIKE GLENN FRANK AND DR. FRANK CRANE ARE NOW REACHING OUT TO THE MENTALITY OF AMERICA AND IN A STRAIGHT MERCHANDISING WAY ARE CARRYING ON MASS EDUCATION.

"THAT FOLLOWING (A), (B), AND (C) WILL COME A SPIRITUALIZATION OF AMERICA. THIS APPLIES NOT SO MUCH IN A RELIGIOUS SENSE BUT RATHER AN APPRECIATION OF ETHICAL VALUES. THIS IS BEING SOLD TO AMERICA TODAY BY EXPONENTS LIKE SWAMI YOGANANDA WHO HAS JUST STARTED TO MERCHANDISE THRU THE PRESS OF AMERICA THE VALUE OF A FULLER AND MORE COMPLETE LIFE, A LIFE SOMEWHERE BETWEEN THE SPIRITUALITY OF CALCUTTA AND THE MATERIALISM OF CHICAGO.

"IT IS MY BELIEF THAT MASS EDUCATION ALONG THESE FOUR LINES IS A NEW PHASE OF JOURNALISM, THE POTENTIALITIES OF WHICH ARE JUST MAKING THEMSELVES FELT AMONG THE NEWSPAPER PUBLISHERS OF THIS CONTINENT."

But what on earth was Yogananda thinking? With America's history of religious idealism, what would make Yogananda think that America needs to be 'spiritualized'? C. S. Lewis had introduced the concept of churchianity vs Christianity, but what would Yogananda have to add to the discussion in America, especially after the hard-won success of Paramananda's efforts. Laurel Keyes details the social stigma and initial ostracization with which Paramananda was initially met. But by the time Yogananda came around much of it had dissipated due to Paramanandaji's influence, especially in the rich and affluent social circles of Washington DC, Boston, and New York City.

Then again what does Kriya yoga have to do with spiritualizing America? Nothing at all, unless you maintain, as Yogananda did for the first 19 years or so that Kriya could be practiced with great success by the members of any and every religion in America, a truly 'creedless teaching,' that requires no conversion from one's given religion.

Certainly this approach is (or would have been) in tune with Lahiri Mahasaya's teaching that a disciple need not leave his family guru or religion in order to practice Kriya.

On the other hand Lahiri's practice "THIS ANONYMOUS AND UNPUBLICIZED WAY -WHAT STRANGE AND UNUSUAL PROPAGATION!" was a contrast to Yogananda's. "HE [LAHIRI] WOULD BE ABSORBED IN YOGA AND GIVE SPIRITUAL COMMENTARIES ON THE GITA AND OTHER BOOKS OF PHILOSOPHY." (Yoga Niketan. A Collection of Biographies of 4 Kriya Yoga Gurus (Kindle Location 511-512). Yoga Niketan, Inc.. Kindle Edition.)

But a closer reading of Paramanandaji's style shows him to be in closer accord with Lahiri than Yogananda. For Paramanandaji close association with him in ashram activities and meditation created saints. That is the time-honored guru-disciple relationship.

"PROFULLA GHOSHAL, A YOUNG HINDU STUDYING WESTERN DRAMA IN NEW YORK CITY, DESCRIBED PARAMANANDA'S APPEARANCE BEFORE 1,200 PEOPLE AT A FELLOWSHIP OF FAITHS MEETING THERE: "WHEN HE CAME IN AND SAT ON THE PLATFORM, THE VERY SIGHT OF HIS SERENE AND YOUTHFUL FACE CALMED MY OVER-STRAINED NERVES." NOR WAS PARAMANANDA SATISFIED SIMPLY TO DISSEMINATE SUCH PEACE FROM THE PODIUM. AS PROFULLA RECORDED: "PERHAPS HE HAD DETECTED MY SUFFERING, FOR HE SAID THAT HE WOULD LIKE TO HAVE ME WITH HIM ALL DAY. I ACTUALLY SPENT THE WHOLE DAY WITH HIM. JUST BEFORE BOARDING THE TRAIN, SWAMIJI SAID: 'WHAT ELSE CAN I DO FOR YOU, PROFULLA?' AND I COULD ONLY REPLY, 'YOU HAVE DONE ENOUGH, SWAMIJI.'" (PP. 264-265, A BRIDGE OF DREAMS)

But Yogananda's efforts began to make it look like one could practice techniques alone (imbibing of course in Yogananda's emphasis on spiritualization of life) without a specific commitment to or need of guru direction. As Yogananda introduced his energization exercises he described them as being inspired or influenced by all the fashionable exercise routines of the day (viz., "My System, Fifteen Minutes a Day for Health Sake," Lt. JP Muller, and Swoboda Course, 1902 by

Alois Swoboda) but with Yogananda's notable emphasis on connecting one's will power to the exercise of specific muscles sets and purposes. (*Yogoda or Tissue-Will System of Physical Perfection*).

Here is an excerpt from a 1946 introduction to Kriya for Indian students that estimates Yogananda's disciple numbers to be close to 300,000! (See Appendix Reference #7 for an excerpt of the 1946 script)

". . . IN 1920 PARAMHANSA (THEN SWAMI) YOGANANDAJI INSPIRED BY THE PROPHETIC WORDS OF HIS MASTER SWAMI SRIYUKTESWAR GIRIJI, CONCERNING THE PROPAGATION [OF] THIS GREAT TEACHING IN AMERICA, LEFT THE BELOVED SHORES AND SPIRITUAL HAVEN OF INDIA TO ATTEND THE INTERNATIONAL CONGRESS OF RELIGIOUS LIBERALS IN BOSTON, MASSACHUSETTS AS THE DELEGATE FROM INDIA . . . DURING HIS SIXTEEN YEARS CONTINUOUS STAY IN AMERICA HE INITIATED NEARLY ONE AND HALF A LAKH [150,000] OF YOGODA DISCIPLES, AND IN THE NEXT DECADE ENDING 1946 THIS NUMBER HAS NEARLY DOUBLED."

Additionally early on in his printing career Yogananda also leaves no distinction in "Yogoda teachings" between the energization exercises and the specific Yogoda meditation techniques (including Kriya). Earlier in this book I pointed out that Yogananda actually gives the 1st Kriya technique as a 'breathing technique' on paragraph 13 of his "Yogoda or Tissue-Will System" booklet!

Nonetheless Yogananda's message was well-received in America. A fellow Indian, Dr. Sudhindra Bose of the University of Iowa, gives the following assessment in the Indian journal "Forward," of Yogananda's message:

"WE ARE TOLD IN A GOOD MANY QUARTERS THAT INDIA SHOULD HAVE HER OWN AGGRESSIVE PROPAGANDISTS IN AMERICA. . . ONE OF THE MOST EFFECTIVE CULTURAL MISSIONARIES WHICH INDIA NOW HAS IN THE UNITED STATES IS SWAMI YOGANANDA. HE HAS A DYNAMIC SPIRITUAL MESSAGE." (P. 27, MAY-JUNE, EAST-WEST MAGAZINE, VOL. III, NO. 4, 1928)

This is an interesting endorsement, and for the 6th issue of East-West Magazine Yogananda poses a question to Dr. Bose' American ("white," non-Indian) wife:

". . . MRS. BOSE WROTE: "YOU WOULD LIKE TO KNOW WHAT I THINK OF MY INDIAN SISTERS. I HAVE A GOOD DEAL OF LOVE, RESPECT AND ADMIRATION FOR THEM, FOR THEIR SWEETNESS AND PATIENCE. SURELY WE IN AMERICA CAN LEARN MUCH FROM THEM, AND I, FOR ONE, DID." (EAST-WEST, 1928, VOL. III, NO. 6, P. 12, SECOND COLUMN).

By 1935 this harmony would be destroyed in the   reaction to Swami
Dhiranandaji's lawsuit. See the chapter "Church Doctrine and Defamation of
Yogananda's Disciples."

Chapter 9. Church Doctrine and Defamation of Yogananda's Disciples

Part of the thrust of this book was to discuss the reasons for my departure from Yogananda's organization, SRF, Inc. In fact I had identified no less than 23 doctrinal issues. But I'm no Martin Luther with 95 theses to pin to the door -- . . . and what's the point?

I suspect realistically that that exercise is futile. Krishna pointed out to a reluctant Arjuna, "WHY DO YOU HESITATE TO KILL THOSE WHO ARE ALREADY DEAD." (Anonymous. Bhagavad-Gita or, The Song Celestial (From the Mahabharata) (mobi) (Penguin Classics) (Kindle Locations 94-96). MobileReference. Kindle Edition.)

I am not interested in railing against SRF, Inc. I see now that it's 'blood line' died with the departures of the two accomplished Kriya masters Yogananda and JJ Lynn (Rajarsi Janakananda); from a 'party line' perspective obviously the disciples of Durga Ma, Kamala Silva, Roy Eugene Davis, Mother Hamilton, Yogacharya Oliver Black, Yogacharya Cuaron, Swami Kriyanandaji, et al. will never be recognized as SRF spiritual heirs. That SRF, Inc. will continue to exist and promote the idea that its 'diksha' transmits the Kriya key, I have no doubt. Why should I "spit into the wind."

Yogananda is no longer in the guru-disciple-making business . . . as Yogananda. That he takes care of his disciples "life after life," I have no doubt. But he's not here with the physical touch. "SRI YUKTESWAR TAUGHT ME HOW TO SUMMON THE BLESSED EXPERIENCE AT WILL, AND ALSO HOW TO TRANSMIT IT TO OTHERS IF THEIR INTUITIVE CHANNELS WERE DEVELOPED." (Yogananda, Paramhansa. Autobiography of a Yogi (Reprint of Original 1946 Edition) (p. 97). Crystal Clarity Publishers - A. Kindle Edition.)

Certainly my experiences with him in this lifetime haven't made me a saint. He visited me (with Lahiri and Sriyukteswar) outside my Dad's parsonage in Astoria, Oregon when I was two. They were very nice to me, waving and smiling as they passed. Later both Yogananda and Sriyukteswarji would come and sit down with me during meditation in my San Antonio home. In the 1995 SRF Convocation both

Yogananda and Sriyukteswar appeared to me during the Kriya initiation service though they didn't speak. I had been on a crying jag during that service, and I overheard Yogananda tell Sriyukteswar that he would return and "take care of him later."

The following year during the 1996 Convocation I suffered a stroke and the neurosurgeon explained to my big brother Bob (himself an ordained minister in the Church of the Nazarene) that she had found a fresh bleed in the cerebral cortex, and that I should be dead or comatose. Perhaps this was Yoganandaji keeping his earlier promise.

But it has been Lahiri Mahasaya who has played wonderfully affectionate games with me over the years. Certainly I understand how the fellow disciple feels when she says that meeting Lahiri in her youth she called him 'grandpa,' and Lahiri would always be that to her.

Not to be divisive but in this line of thinking the times that Lord Jesus has visited me never ever has he demanded that I 'accept him as Lord and Savior.' To me he is a most trusted friend.

So if I were to 'take on' SRF, Inc., it might imply that I acknowledge the legitimacy of its *Kriya* mission, or that I believe its mission can somehow be a channel for the guru-disciple *diksha*. That it can do good in this world, I have no doubt; "more power to them," is my blessing.

'Dog and Pony Show' Travels America to Spread Kriya

However I do have an interest in the 'dog and pony' show that Yogananda put on for American audiences to spread his ideas of what the "Master Minds of India" are thinking. This approach started about a year after Dhiranandaji arrived in Boston.

For this new approach Yogananda used an advance man known as

1. Captain Rashid whom he'd met on the ocean voyage to America,
2. An Italian circus man Hamid Bey whom Yogananda billed as the miracle man from Egypt who could stop his respiratory system and heart beat in front of audiences, and
3. Dr. Roman Ostoja allegedly billed as "Count" Ostoja of Polish extraction; he was actually from Cleveland, Ohio. He also claimed ability to control respiratory and cardiac systems. In one of these demonstrations with Leo Tolstoy in which Roman was buried alive, Tolstoy's wife Sofia for whatever reason insisted his body be dug up before the experiment was to have been concluded. Allegedly Roman was suffocating, and her intervention saved his life. I am aware of one of his books, *Body and Mind Control*, 1949, JF Rowny Press, Santa Barbara, Ca.

Calling it a 'dog and pony show' is a way to avoid accusing Yogananda of outright lies and deception; this way it was just entertainment to get America's attention.

Nawabzada Muhammed Rashid

Swami Satyananda gives information about Muhammed Rashid:

UP TO 1924, THE WORK WENT ON WITH BOSTON AS THE CENTER. AT A CERTAIN TIME, A YOUTH NAMED MOHAMMED RASHID ARRIVED AT SWAMIJI'S PLACE, AFTER HAVING FINISHED HIS STUDIES AT AN AMERICAN UNIVERSITY. I HAVE HEARD FROM RASHID THAT HE WAS ACTUALLY A FELLOW PASSENGER FROM CALCUTTA WITH SWAMIJI [DURING HIS JOURNEY TO AMERICA]. HE WAS DRAWN TO SWAMIJI FROM THAT VERY TIME, BUT NOT MUCH INTERACTION HAPPENED. HE WENT ON TO CONTINUE HIS STUDIES. AFTER THE COMPLETION OF HIS STUDIES, HE SEARCHED OUT SWAMIJI, CAME TO BOSTON, BECAME HIS DISCIPLE, AND INSTIGATED SWAMIJI TO LEAVE THE BOUNDARIES OF BOSTON, TRAVEL THE HUGE AMERICAN LAND, AND SPREAD   THE MESSAGE THROUGHOUT. AN AUTOMOBILE WAS FOUND. TWO OTHER YOUTHS CAME ALONG AS COMPANIONS AND ATTENDANTS. MOHAMMED RASHID HIMSELF BECAME SWAMIJI'S SECRETARY. THE OTHER YOUTHS BECAME DRIVERS OF THE AUTOMOBILE. DURING THIS AUSPICIOUS JOURNEY, HE WENT AROUND GIVING LECTURES IN DIFFERENT CITIES. YOGA NIKETAN. A COLLECTION OF BIOGRAPHIES OF 4 KRIYA YOGA GURUS (KINDLE LOCATIONS 4023-4029). YOGA NIKETAN, INC.. KINDLE EDITION.

Yogananda published an article by Rashid, "Thoughts From Sufism," East-West Magazine, Vol. 1, No 2, p. 11, Jan-Feb 1925-1926.

Later that year Yogananda bid farewell to Rashid in the article "Mr. Rashid Visits India," East-West Magazine, 1925-26, Volume I, No. 6, p28. Satyanandaji, on the other hand gives an intriguing account of Rashid's leave, claiming

"MR. RASHID, SWAMIJI'S WORKING-SECRETARY, CAME TO INDIA TO MANAGE THE DEPARTURE OF WORKERS FROM HERE. HE WAS INVITED TO BOTH CALCUTTA AND RANCHI." (YOGA NIKETAN. A COLLECTION OF BIOGRAPHIES OF 4 KRIYA YOGA GURUS (KINDLE LOCATION 4092). YOGA NIKETAN, INC.. KINDLE EDITION.)

Rashid apparently recommended just the one young Indian Brahmachari Jotin (who would later become Swami Premananda) to come to America to assist Yogananda. He left Mother Center in 1926, but it was two more years before his recommended Indian youth arrived to assist Yogananda.

The singular picture of Rashid is from East-West Vol I No 2, 1925-26, Jan-Feb, p. 72. It accompanies an announcement of Rashid's successful translation of "the immortal masterpiece "Shama Aur Shair" or "Candle and Poet," by the Persian poet, Sir M. Iqbal." In that announcement Rashid is addressed as Nawabzada M. Rashid. Approximately 18 months later the East-West Vol III No 1, 1926-27 Nov-Dec, pp. 23-24 announce his return to the United States, and mentions that Rashid has promised to provide in a future East-West magazine an article describing his tour of the Yogoda schools that he visited while in India.

Here is an undated picture with Rashid, Sri Nerode, Yoganandaji, et al. Rashid is to Nerode's left.

Hamid Bey

Yogananda writes of Hamid Bey in EAST WEST Magazine, September—
October, 1927 VOL. 2—6. Pp. 26-27:

. . .MR. BEY'S FEATS ARE PERFORMED. . . BY MANIPULATING GLANDS OF THE THROAT AND BY
PRESSING CERTAIN NERVES ON THE HEAD. THESE ARE VERY INTERESTING PHYSIOLOGICAL PHENOMENA
SHOWING THAT MAN CAN CONTROL THE FUNCTIONS OF THE HEART AND ALL OTHER ORGANS OF
INVOLUNTARY ACTION. THIS IS KNOWN TO HINDU YOGIS AND SWAMIS WHO PRACTICE YOGA, AS
WELL AS TO MYSTICS OF OTHER SECTS.

OF COURSE, IT MUST BE REMEMBERED THAT WITHOUT THE LOVE OF GOD AND WITHOUT
WISDOM, SUCH CONTROL AND FEATS ARE JUST PHYSIOLOGICAL JUGGLERY AND A DETRIMENT TO
SPIRITUAL REALIZATION. BUT HAMID BEY LOVES GOD . . .

I TOLD MR. BEY TO PRODUCE TRANCE BY LOVE OF GOD, RATHER THAN MERELY BY GLANDULAR
PRESSURE, AS RESULTS PRODUCED BY DEVOTION ARE SAFER AND GREATER. GENERALLY, IT TAKES
ANOTHER PERSON TO AROUSE MR. BEY FROM HIS TRANCE. BUT, IN THE CONSCIOUS TRANCE OF
DEVOTION, OR YOGA, ONE NEVER LOSES CONSCIOUSNESS BUT TRANSCENDS THE MATERIAL
CONSCIOUSNESS AND COMES BACK TO CONSCIOUSNESS OF MATTER AT WILL AGAIN. THAT IS THE
CONSCIOUS COMMUNION WITH GOD THE YOGODA ASPIRES TO TEACH.

Later Hamid was chosen to teach Yogoda at various locations, and Sri Nerode
on occasion accompanied him on these more appropriate tours. I do not know if
Hamid was given authority to give Kriya initiation.

Though Sri Nerode and Hamid stayed in touch (by letter), there came a time
when Hamid was separated from the Yogoda work.

For this purpose Gyanamataji notified Sri Nerode by letter dated June 13th
1935,

". . . SWAMIJI WAS INFORMED OF YOGI HAMID BEY'S DISHONESTY, AND OUR LAWYER HAS
BEEN INSTRUCTED BY HIM TO COMMENCE SUIT AGAINST THE YOGI.

"WE WERE VERY GLAD THAT SRIMATI MENTIONED THE CITY WHERE HE IS, AS THAT WAS THE
FIRST THING OUR LAWYER WANTED TO KNOW. I CANNOT AT THIS TIME TELL YOU JUST WHAT CAN BE
DONE. WE ARE GATHERING ALL THE COPYRIGHTS TOGETHER. "

In this letter Sister Gyanamataji informed Sri Nerode about Yogananda suing
Bey for 'dishonesty.' From her letter it appears that maybe both Sri and Srimata
Nerode are the ones who informed Yoganandaji about Hamid Bey's behavior. (See
Reference section for the unOCR'd letter, #17. Gyanamataji's Letter to Sri Nerode about Hamid Bey)

I find no more information about Hamid Bey other than the booklet *HAMID BEY, "MIRACLE MAN"*. Although the booklet lists Swami Yogananda as the author, I received an email from Rod Richmond acknowledging that the booklet is his combination of various pieces of information regarding Yogananda and Bey's relationship. The document says nothing about Bey's parting from Yogananda.

(See the Appendix Reference for a copy of Hamid's US naturalization application showing his former nationality as Italian rather than Egyptian as claimed by Yogananda)

Satyeswarananda refers to him as a man of Arabic decent. On page 980 he prints a handwritten letter from Yogananda to Nerode (dated Oct. 17 but no specific year) in which Yogananda writes, "YOGI IS DOING NO GOOD BUT HARM. YOU ARE DOING REAL GOOD THIS IS THE TRUTH. WITH THE AMERICANS MANAGERS YOGI IS TURNING OUT A COMMERCIAL MAN – I WILL TELL YOU WHEN I MEET YOU. SY"

In the benediction of this same letter ironically he commends to Nerode his white wife, Agnes, "SO GLAD SHE STANDS BY YOU LIKE A REAL HINDU WIFE."

Roman Ostoja

In the back of his 1949 2nd edition book (*Body and Mind Control*) I find the following endorsement by Yogananda:

"READ WHAT NOTABLES AND AUTHORITIES SAY ABOUT DOCTOR OSTOJA'S WORK

"DEAR FRIENDS:

"I CONSIDER YOGI ROMAN OSTOJA ONE OF THE GREAT DIVINE HEALERS OF MODERN TIMES. I PREFER HIM TO TEN THOUSAND SPIRITUAL TEACHERS WHO CAN TALK BUT CANNOT DEMONSTRATE SPIRITUAL TRUTHS.

"HE IS A WESTERNER WHO HAS STUDIED WITH SOME OF THE GREAT MASTERS OF INDIA, AND HE HAS ALSO REINFORCED HIS STUDIES WITH ME. YOGI OSTOJA WILL PROVE TO YOU THAT PEOPLE OF THE OCCIDENT CAN ALSO MASTER THE UNIVERSAL TEACHINGS OF INDIA.

"I HAVE FOUND YOGI OSTOJA DURING MY PAST YEAR'S ASSOCIATION WITH HIM. DOING EXTRAORDINARY HEALING AND TEACHING WORK AND GIVING NEW TEACHINGS WHICH HAVE REVOLUTIONIZED THE LIVES OF MANY PERSONS AND WHICH, I AM SURE, WILL GIVE YOU THE POWER TO CREATE AT WILL WHAT YOU NEED. HIS CLASSES ARE ESPECIALLY REMARKABLE BENEFICIAL."

"WITH UNCEASING BLESSINGS,

"PARAMHANSA YOGANANDA"

In the 1937 Inner Culture East-West magazine Ostoja is listed as an SRF minister. (Volume IX, No. 5). His leadership as teacher at the Cleveland, Ohio location is mentioned on p. 44; he has a one page article "Joyousness" published on p. 65 which is actually the speech he gave at the January 1937 Banquet welcoming Yogananda home from India.

I find no information regarding the breakup of their business efforts. Here are pictures in which Ostoja demonstrates his mastery of the body:

The defamation section deals with four of Yogananda's Associates: Ranendra Kumar Das, Swami Dhirananda, Sri Nerode, and Swami Kriyananda.

Swami Kriyanandaji

I am more interested in Yogananda's style of defaming those who chose to leave his Yogoda mission. Whatever SRF, Inc. does now by way of assessing the character of previous disciples, I can only conclude that they learned well from their mentor, Yogananda.

Of course I am speaking of Swami Kriyananda, former Vice-President of SRF, Inc., who took Dr. Lewis' place on the Board of Directors in 1960. Yogananda did not defame him, but it appears that SRF, Inc. continues to borrow a page or two from Yogananda's machinations to continue what I think USC's Josiah Royce would call an "existential lie" about Donald K. Walters in the way SRF, Inc. framed both Kriyananda's departure from SRF, Inc. and his continued discipleship. With the recent change of leadership at SRF, Inc., I do hope that Swami Chidanandaji is "man enough" to acknowledge and stop the unwarranted attacks on Swami Kriyananda, just as Chidanandaji was "man enough" to say "no" to the SRF, Inc. Attorney Michael Flynn, as Ananda defense attorney Jon Parson's points out:

"FLYNN THROWN OUT OF COURT | OCTOBER 2002
"DURING THE MORNING BREAK ON ONE OF THE FIRST DAYS OF TESTIMONY, I WAS WALKING DOWN THE WINDOW-WALLED CORRIDOR OUTSIDE OUR EIGHTH-FLOOR COURTROOM WHEN I HEARD FLYNN'S LOUD AND UNMISTAKABLE VOICE. IT WAS BOOMING THROUGH THE OPEN DOOR OF AN ATTORNEY CONFERENCE ROOM. "JUST SAY NO! THAT'S ALL YOU HAVE TO DO, JUST SAY NO!" AS I WALKED PAST I TURNED MY HEAD AND SAW FLYNN HARANGUING BROTHER CHIDANANDA, THE WITNESS THEN STILL IN THE MIDDLE OF TESTIFYING, WHO WOULD RETAKE THE STAND IMMEDIATELY AFTER THE BREAK. IT MAY SURPRISE SOME, BUT THERE ARE LIMITS TO THE ETHICAL COACHING OF WITNESSES, CALLED "WOODSHEDDING," AND IT SOUNDED LIKE FLYNN HAD CROSSED THAT LINE. WHAT SURPRISED ME, THOUGH, WAS THAT HE DID IT SHOUTING AT A WITNESS IN A SMALL ROOM WITH AN OPEN DOOR OFF THE HALLWAY NEXT TO THE COURTROOM. WHAT DOES THAT TELL YOU? THE DOOR WIDE OPEN. COMPOUNDING THE FOLLY WAS THE FACT THAT [PRESIDING FEDERAL JUDGE] GARCIA HAD ALREADY TAKEN THE TROUBLE OF PROHIBITING FLYNN FROM OFFICIALLY APPEARING AS SRF'S COUNSEL IN THE CASE. FLYNN COULD NOT REPRESENT SRF IN THE COURTROOM, YET HERE HE WAS, TELLING AN SRF WITNESS WHAT TO SAY WHEN HE RESUMED TESTIFYING.

AS AN OFFICER OF THE COURT I HAD   THE . . . DUTY OF BRINGING SUCH EGREGIOUS MISBEHAVIOR TO GARCIA'S ATTENTION. HIS HONOR WAS UPSET. . . GARCIA CALLED FLYNN FORWARD, AND . . . GARCIA . . . ASKED WHETHER THIS WAS THE SAME MICHAEL FLYNN THE JUDGE HAD EARLIER PROHIBITED FROM APPEARING AS *PRO HAC* VICE COUNSEL IN THE CASE. THE EXCHANGE TURNED UGLY, WITH . . . GARCIA EJECTING FLYNN FROM THE COURTROOM. . ." (A FIGHT FOR RELIGIOUS FREEDOM: A LAWYER'S PERSONAL ACCOUNT OF COPYRIGHTS, KARMA AND DHARMIC LITIGATION, OCTOBER 16, 2012, JON R. PARSONS (AUTHOR); CRYSTAL CLARITY, PUBLISHERS)

Not one single piece of damning evidence has ever been produced by SRF, Inc. to justify Kriyanandaji's dismissal from SRF, Inc. Not one; and that has left a vacuum for rumors, gossip, lies, and distortions to be committed by "purist" devotees of SRF, Inc. This is what I dub the "existential lie." Most accusations go to Kriyananda's presumed sexual misbehavior; most of those who take that path have no knowledge that Kriyanandaji discussed with Daya Mataji his consensual sexual encounter with an SRF nun in 1955 . . . and yet five years later he was elected as Vice-President of the SRF Board.

Those purists apparently know nothing of Yogananda's sexual behavior; or of written eyewitness accounts which are presented in this book.

Yogananda's Machinations – lawsuit threats, slander, and losing paperwork

Yogananda speaks to Durga Ma (Fiona Darling) about the importance of threats of lawsuits to discourage people from opposing him.

"April-6-1936----. . , about settling the lawsuit, you know best what to do and we will be glad if it is over soon, if it is over [Sudhindra] Bose will have less cause to criticize . . . he must be kept in fear of being sued, he got Dhirananda to write a nasty impersonal article about all Swamis in one [of the] best magazines, "Modern Review" and . . . we have built powerful newspaper and other friends . . ."

And in a letter to James J Lynn recorded by Durga Ma Yogananda writes,

"AUGUST 22, 1945 – EVEN JESUS HAD HIS JUDAS, AND MY HUMBLE SELF HAD HIS JUDASES IN DHIRANANDA AND NERODE . . ." (A Paramhansa Yogananda Trilogy of Divine Love)

As will be seen Gyanamataji apparently saw beyond her guru's hyperbole. In that same June 13 1935 (See #17 in the Appendix Reference) letter cited above she observes at the end of the 4th paragraph that "ONE CANNOT CARRY ON PERPETUAL LAWSUITS." Later her loyalty to Sri and Srimati Nerode and their child Sri Anil will be shown in another letter after Yogananda leads a 'palace coup' to drive them away.

Ranendra Kumar Das

One of the few disciples that Yogananda did not defame upon his departure from Yogoda was the Indian Ranendra Kumar Das who had been so long at the Indianapolis Yogoda Center. Durga Ma says,

"[RANENDRA] COMPLAINED TO MASTER THAT I DID NOTHING ELSE BUT SEND THOSE LETTERS [WITH FAMINE RELIEF MONEY FOR INDIA] AND I SHOULD DO OTHER WORK INSTEAD. MASTER ANSWERED HIM, "THAT IS THE REASON I PLACED HER IN THAT DEPARTMENT TO DO MY WISHES, SINCE YOU DON'T WANT TO DO IT." DAS . . . TRIED TO FRIGHTEN MASTER BY SAYING, "ALL RIGHT THEN, PUT HER IN CHARGE OF THE OFFICE, I AM LEAVING." MASTER IMMEDIATELY TOOK HIM UP ON THAT, AND DAS ANSWERED, "ALL RIGHT, I WILL." (A Paramhansa Yogananda Trilogy of Love)

Ranendra was well educated and the author of several fine books, two of which I have republished: "Reincarnation," and "It Can Done."

I still receive inquiries from loving devotees at his previous SRF Center in Indianapolis.

Swami Dhiranandaji

Contrary to the usual narrative about Yogananda preferring Swami Satyananda to come and assist him in America, Swami Satyananda claims that Yogananda had said from America,

"SO, EITHER DHIRANANDA OR SATYANANDA, ONE OF THE TWO OF YOU WILL HAVE TO COME HERE TO JOIN IN THIS WORK WITH HUGE POTENTIAL. BOTH OF YOU, BE READY. WHOMEVER I CALL WILL HAVE TO COME WITHOUT DELAY." Yoga Niketan. A Collection of Biographies of 4 Kriya Yoga Gurus (Kindle Locations 3988-3990). Yoga Niketan, Inc., Kindle Edition.

The usual narrative has made it sound like using Dhirananda was a doomed exercise.

"WE ALSO GAVE DHIRANANDAJI A FOND FAREWELL AND PUT HIM ON THE SHIP IN CALCUTTA. BECAUSE OF A PARTICULAR OBSTACLE, GURU MAHARAJ JI [SWAMI SRIYUKTESWAR] WAS NOT ABLE TO COME TO THE DOCKS. LATER, HE SAID SOMEWHAT QUIETLY AND SOMBERLY THAT HE FELT THAT THE BEGINNING OF AN INAUSPICIOUS FUTURE WAS CONNECTED WITH THIS JOURNEY THAT DHIRANANDA WAS TAKING. DHIRANANDAJI REACHED BOSTON AFTER ONE MONTH." (Yoga Niketan. A Collection of Biographies of 4 Kriya Yoga Gurus (Kindle Locations 4017-4019). Yoga Niketan, Inc., Kindle Edition.)

I even recall Yogananda claiming that he had known from childhood that his childhood friend, later Swami Dhirananda, would betray him.

But what is the actual narrative? Dhirananda came to America at Yogananda's request, worked in Boston for a couple years sustaining himself by teaching at various colleges while running Yogoda affairs, and then handled Mother Center business (including lecturing) with the same acumen as he had shown at Ranchi while Yogananda took the lecture tour. Satyananda recounts that Dhirananda had an MA degree

"AND BECAME A PH.D., AND IS PRESENTLY AN EMINENT PROFESSOR IN THE UNIVERSITY OF MICHIGAN IN AMERICA." Yoga Niketan. A Collection of Biographies of 4 Kriya Yoga Gurus (Kindle Locations 2740-2741). Yoga Niketan, Inc., Kindle Edition.

Dhiranandaji's ship manifest shows he sailed from Calcutta July 22, 1922 (#11 in the Appendix Reference); his family name is listed as Basukumar Bagchi and given name is Giri. Satyananada-giri states that

"BASUKUMAR WAS INITIATED INTO KRIYA YOGA BY SHASTRI MAHASAYA." Yoga Niketan. A Collection of Biographies of 4 Kriya Yoga Gurus (Kindle Location 2736). Yoga Niketan, Inc., Kindle Edition.

Yogananda gives a glowing endorsement of Dhiranandaji in the inaugural volume of East-West magazine (Volume I 1925-1926, No. 1, p. 29, November-December, 1925) (See Reference Appendix #12)

I AM POWERLESS TO TELL HOW GREATLY HE HAS HELPED ME IN CARRYING ON MY EDUCATIONAL WORK IN INDIA AND BOSTON OR OF THE GOOD WHICH THE WORLD HAS DERIVED FROM HIS IDEAL CHARACTER AND EXALTED SPIRITUAL LIFE. HE WILL BLESS MOUNT WASHINGTON WITH HIS PRESENCE THERE AS THE RESIDENTIAL SWAMI. JUST AS HE SUCCESSFULLY CARRIED ON THE WORK OF THE RANCHI SCHOOL DURING THE FIRST TWO YEARS OF MY ABSENCE FROM INDIA, SO WILL HE LIKEWISE TAKE CHARGE OF THE LOS ANGELES HEADQUARTERS WHENEVER I AM OF NECESSITY ABSENT FROM THERE ON LECTURE TOURS FOR THE SPREAD OF GOD'S MESSAGE OF ALL-ROUND EDUCATION AND HUMAN PERFECTION.

SWAMI DHIRANANDA WILL CONDUCT A SUNDAY SCHOOL CLASS FOR BOYS AND GIRLS EVERY SUNDAY MORNING AT MOUNT WASHINGTON, AND ATTEND TO THE WORK OF THE YOGODA CORRESPONDENCE COURSE, AS WELL AS CARRY ON FURTHER SPIRITUAL WORK AS IT DEVELOPS.

Dhirananda was a scholar and an author of many books over his lifetime. Yogananda acknowledges that he owes Dhirananda for his literary work on the Indian edition of *Science of Religion* from which Yogananda read his talk to the Congress of Religious Liberals in Boston. (See Appendix Reference #13)

While working for Yogoda in the Boston area from late 1922 through the 1925 acquisition of the Los Angeles property, Dhirananda provided his own keep through teaching.

Satyananda supports this detail:

SWAMIJI [YOGANANDA] . . . BEGAN TO MAKE PREPARATIONS TO SET UP THE MAIN CENTER IN LOS ANGELES. BY THAT TIME, DHIRANANDAJI HAD ESTABLISHED HIMSELF QUITE WELL IN BOSTON IN THE AREA OF TEACHING AND MATHEMATICS, BUT AT LEADER YOGANANDAJI'S WISHES, HE SHUT EVERYTHING DOWN, WENT TO MOUNT WASHINGTON IN LOS ANGELES, AND TOOK ON THE RESPONSIBILITY OF THAT CENTER. YOGANANDAJI - AS WAS IN HIS NATURE - WENT ON TRAVELING AND PROPAGATING THE MESSAGE. YOGA NIKETAN. A COLLECTION OF BIOGRAPHIES OF 4 KRIYA YOGA GURUS (KINDLE LOCATIONS 4032-4036). YOGA NIKETAN, INC.. KINDLE EDITION.

Srimati Nerode allows that Dhirananda was the sole author of *The Science of Religion*, writer of the *12 lesson Yogoda lessons*, and partial author with Yogananda of *Songs of the Soul*. (See Appendix References #19 and #20, *Memoirs of Srimati Nerode, Interview with Srimati Nerode;* see the list of some of his books, #24.)

So how does it happen that Yogananda begins calling Dhiranandaji a 'judas.'?

Dhirananda had plenty of opportunity to tell his side of the story. All I have seen in 40 years with SRF, Inc. is that 'of a sudden' [my choice of words] Yogananda signed a promissory note to Dhirananda on April 11, 1929 for $8,000 payable in $100.00 monthly installments. In the event of non-payment five months in a row, the remaining sum would become due. Yogananda appeared before Terese M. Lindfeldt, Notary Public, Kings County Clerk No. 213, Register No. 339. N. Y. County Clerk No. 472, Register No. 0-334 (See Appendix Reference #6).

Yogananda made one $100.00 payment (the month following the date of this note). By 1935 he had made no more payments.

SRF, Inc. gives no rationale for Yogananda taking on such promissory note. At least I hadn't seen one in my 40 years of being a purist believer in SRF, Inc.

LAUREL KEYES DESCRIBES DHIRANANDA AS A MAN WHO LIKES FACTS. IT WOULD BE DOUBTFUL IF I WOULD HAVE LEARNED AS MUCH IF I HAD GONE TO LIVE IN INDIA. INDIA HAD COME TO ME, IN THREE PERSONS. PARAMANANDA WAS THE MYSTIC -- THE EXAMPLE, THE IDEAL HUMAN, DEVOTED TO HIS GOD, PRACTICAL, ADAPTABLE, BLENDING PRAYERS AND GARDENING, BUILDING AND WISE COUNSELING ALL TOGETHER. YOGANANDA WAS A TRADITIONAL HOLY MAN. DHIRANANDA WAS A TEACHER -- EAGER, CURIOUS, ALWAYS DEMANDING "PROOF" AND ALWAYS EXCITED ABOUT SOME NEW OR OLD CONCEPT. IT WAS HE PERHAPS WHO FIRST GAVE THE PHRASE, "I HAVE NO FAITH IN BELIEF, AND DON'T BELIEVE IN FAITH. THERE MUST BE PROOF!" (SUNDIAL, I COUNT THE SUNNY HOURS, LAUREL ELIZABETH KEYES, GENTLE LIVING PUBLICATIONS, 1982 2ND PRINTING, PP. 100-104 AD PASSIM)

Apparently Dhirananda had heard rumors in 1929 about Yogananda and Laurie Pratt living together in New York. Dhirananda flew up there, as I understand the narrative, lived with Yogananda and Laurie for three days convincing himself of the truth of the rumors.

Dhirananda demanded payment for his contributions to the work that he felt Yogananda had betrayed by his sexual behavior. Yogananda signed the promissory note before the notary public in Kings County, New York City. Dhirananda returned to Los Angeles, and separated himself from the Yogoda work.

As noted above, Yogananda made the first and only payment of $100.00 when due the following month. To paraphrase *Judge Judy*, Yogananda's payment (let alone his signature on the note) indicates Yogananda's acknowledgement of the debt; important point because Yogananda later has his attorney claim in court that Dhiranandaji forged his signature!

Dhirananda made no public denouncements of Yogananda at the time he left Yogoda. At least I haven't seen any. He still had his spiritual idealism, and attempted to start an organization of his own in Los Angeles. That didn't succeed, and he decided to renounce his renunciate vows altogether. As far as I have found Yogananda did not publicly denounce Dhirananda at the time of their split-up.

Keyes describes it simply;

Differences grew between Yogananda and Dhirananda so that a separation took place. Dhirananda renounced his religious vocation, took his family name and went to University of Iowa where he earned his Ph. D. and became one of the pioneers in Electro-encephalogram research. (IBID.)

Laurel had received Kriya initiation from Swami Dhiranandaji. In her gentle way Laurel describes what happened over the years:

"IT ISN'T POSSIBLE TO DESCRIBE FRIENDSHIPS AND HOW THEY FORM. IT IS MORE LIKE ACCEPTING SOMETHING ALREADY EXISTING. TARA HAD SEEMED TO HAVE BEEN MY SISTER ALWAYS. WE STUDIED TOGETHER. WE ATTENDED LECTURE TOGETHER AND WHEN IT WAS TIME FOR ME TO TAKE MY KRIYA INITIATION FROM DHIRANANDA, TARA WAS THERE.

"LATER, THEY [THE FORMER DHIRANANDA AND EVA GLADYS WEBBER, AKA TARA] WERE MARRIED IN OUR HOME IN DENVER AND THEY REMAINED A PART OF MY FAMILY OVER THE YEARS. (OUR PHILOSOPHICAL AND RELIGIOUS VIEWS MAY NOT ALWAYS HAVE BEEN IN FULL AGREEMENT BUT WE HAVE ALWAYS LOVED ONE ANOTHER)

"YOGANANDA'S NAME IS KNOWN AROUND THE WORLD FOR HIS AUTOBIOGRAPHY OF A YOGI. DR. BASU KUMAR BAGCHI, (FORMERLY DHIRANANDA) PROFESSOR EMERITUS AT UNIVERSITY OF MICHIGAN, IS PERHAPS AS WELL KNOWN IN THE FIELD OF BRAIN WAVE RESEARCH. ONE AFTERNOON, AFTER HE HAD RETIRED, HE AND TARA TOOK ME TO THE LITTLE BASEMENT ROOM WHICH HE HAD USED FOR HIS FIRST LABORATORY, A WINDOWLESS, DISMAL BACKROOM IN WHICH HE WAS RELEGATED TO PROVE HIS THEORIES ABOUT DIAGNOSTIC AND THERAPEUTIC BENEFITS — AT THAT TIME 35 YEARS BEFORE, A DOUBTFUL AND CONTROVERSIAL FIELD.

"THEN HE WALKED OUT AND THROUGH THE ENTIRE WING OF A NEW BUILDING WHICH HAD BEEN CONSTRUCTED TO HOUSE THE LIFE-TIME WORK HE HAD STARTED. OUTSIDE I STOPPED TO VIEW IT, THRILLED AT WHAT SATISFACTION THIS MUST BRING HIM.

"KUMAR — LOOK WHAT YOU HAVE ACCOMPLISHED! YOU SET OUT TO PROVE CERTAIN ANCIENT EASTERN CONCEPTS SCIENTIFICALLY AND NOW YOGA AND EASTERN PHILOSOPHIES ARE SO

INTERLACED IN OUR CULTURE THAT WE ACCEPT THEM AS HAVING LONG BEEN WITH US. THINK WHAT PART YOU HAD IN WHAT HAS HAPPENED."

"TYPICAL OF THE SEEKING, PROBING, NEVER-SATISFIED MIND, KUMAR SHRUGGED, "I DON'T KNOW WHETHER MY LITTLE CONTRIBUTION HAS DONE ANYTHING REALLY. THERE IS STILL SO MUCH TO KNOW, TO DISCOVER, TO PROVE —" (IBID.)

In the Reference section I have placed an excerpt of the unOCR'd copy of the memoriam to Tara (Eva Gladys Webber) as well as a published Tribute to Dr. Bagchi's 1957 Brain Research. (See #14 and #15 in Appendix Reference)

The promissory note between Yogananda and Dhirananda allowed for pursuit of the full amount due if payments are not made over five months. After five more months of non-payments, Dhiranandaji filed suit in 1929 in Los Angeles, but the file was lost in the Courthouse after the filing. Dhiranandaji went on with his life instead, obtaining his Ph. D. from the University of Iowa, getting married, conducting pioneering brain-wave research, etc. By 1935 Yogananda had made only the one payment. Dr. Bagchi decided to sue for the $7900.00 balance.

Dr. Bagchi had had enough of Yogananda's attempts to undermine his Ph.D. program (Yogananda twice visited the University of Iowa while Bagchi was a candidate for the Ph.D.) or to otherwise continue non-payment on the valid debt. He not only left for India in 1935 shortly after refiling the lawsuit but published this article about the time that Yogananda would have been arriving there.

"THE GREATEST TRAGEDY, HOWEVER, DOES NOT COME FROM THESE PSYCHICS BUT FROM THOSE WHOM THEY CONSIDER AS OLDER BRETHREN IN THE TRADE. THEY ARE THE SWAMIS, YOGIS, RISHIS OR FREELANCE LECTURERS AND LIBERATORS AT LARGE. THEY ARE "INTELLECTUALS"; SOMETIMES THEY HAVE A DEGREE OR TWO FROM SOME UNIVERSITIES. THEY HAVE A FACILE TONGUE, PRETENTIOUS IDEALISM, CUNNING MANNERS, ORANGE ROBES AND SOMETIMES LONG HAIR. FROM THE PLATFORM THEY EITHER SHRIEK[SIC], SWEAR AND SCOLD, OR ORATE, CHANT AND MYSTIFY. IF DIFFERENT, THEY POSIT JUST A SAINTLY "HALO." PROBABLY THEY REPRESENT SOME TINY RELIGIOUS ORGANIZATION OF INDIA; SOMETIMES THEY ARE SELF-STYLED PRESIDENTS OF THEIR OWN ORGANIZATION. THEY HAVE ADOPTED THE HIGH-POWERED SALESMANSHIP OF AMERICAN BUSINESS TO BOOST THEIR COURSE OF PHILOSOPHIC AND RELIGIOUS TEACHING TO SPIRITUALLY HUNGRY AND NERVOUSLY SICK AMERICAN MEN AND WOMEN, MOSTLY WOMEN, USING SUCH BAIT PHRASES AS "MARVELOUS ILLUMINATION," "INSTANTANEOUS HEALING," "GOD-CONSCIOUSNESS," AND CHARGING EACH FROM 25 TO 100 DOLLARS FOR THEIR COURSES OF LESSONS. THEY HIRE HALLS AT DIFFERENT CITIES, GIVE FREE LECTURES FOR A WEEK OR SO LAUDING THEIR COURSES TO THE SKIES AND YET CLEVERLY PHRASING THEIR PROMISES SO AS NOT TO GET INTO LEGAL COMPLICATIONS WITH THE GOVERNMENT. THEN PEOPLE PAY COLD CASH FOR ONE COURSE AFTER ANOTHER ON CALISTHENIC

EXERCISES TO SUPER-ADVANCED METAPHYSICS, PRANIC PHYSICAL CULTURE TO HIGHEST VIBRATORY HEALING. AT THE END OF A MONTH OR A YEAR A FEW OF THEM REVOLT FOR BEING CHEATED, A FEW THINK THEY HAVE RECEIVED BENEFIT BECAUSE THEY HAVE PAID FOR IT, A FEW KEEP QUIET FOR THEIR FOOLISHNESS, AND A FEW "LOYAL" SOULS CARRY ON THE BANNER BECAUSE THEY FEEL THEY HAVE GOT WHAT THEY HAVE BEEN LOOKING FOR YEARS. THE MASTER SWAMI (WE WONDER WHENCE THE ADJECTIVE MASTER SPRANG) OR THE LIBERATOR AFTER A STAY OF A MONTH OR SO MOVES ON TO CONQUER NEW TERRITORY LEAVING SOMEBODY IN CHARGE OF THE OLD. THEIR STUDENTS RUN FROM 30 TO 1500 IN NUMBER, NETTING THE GURU FROM SIX HUNDRED TO TWENTY-FIVE THOUSAND DOLLARS IN EACH PLACE. AND THE SHREWD AMERICAN SIGHS, "ANOTHER RACKET!"

THE SWAMI HAS AN EAGER EYE FOR NEWSPAPER PUBLICITY BUT HE WOULD RATHER NOT TAKE CARE OF SUCH MUNDANE MATTERS HIMSELF. HE LETS HIS ADVANCE AGENT DO THAT FOR HIM WHEN A NEW TERRITORY IS INVADED. OF COURSE, LESSER SWAMIS CANNOT AFFORD THE LUXURY OF A FIVE- TO SIX-THOUSAND-DOLLAR-A-YEAR ADVANCE AGENT. THESE AGENTS PROCURE A LIST OF WEALTHY MEN AND WOMEN, ESPECIALLY WIDOWS, AND THE SWAMI WORMS HIS WAY INTO THEIR CONFIDENCES TO RELIEVE THEM OF THEIR EARTHLY TREASURE IN EXCHANGE FOR SPIRITUAL BLESSINGS. SOMETIMES HIS STUDENTS INCLUDE FAMOUS PERSONAGES, SUCH AS SYMPHONY ORCHESTRA CONDUCTORS, OPERA SINGERS, SOCIETY MATRONS AND DOCTORS FROM WHOM HE MANAGES TO GET TESTIMONIALS WHEN THE LESSONS ARE FRESH AND HOT IN THEIR MINDS BECAUSE OF THE MAGIC PRESENCE OF THE DIVINE SAVANT. A FEW OF THESE HE SELECTS FOR CLOSER ASSOCIATION, AND LET NONE BE SO UNSPIRITUAL AS TO THINK THAT THIS ASSOCIATION HAS ANYTHING TO DO WITH SOAKING UP THEIR PRESTIGE! THE TESTIMONIALS ARE PRINTED IN THE FREE LITERATURE AND THE MAGAZINE OF THE SWAMIS, AND THE UNENQUIRING INDIAN AND AMERICAN PUBLIC EXCLAIMS, "WHAT A MAN!" THE TRUTH OF THE MATTER IS THAT AMERICANS ARE, AS A RULE, GOOD SPORTSMEN, THEY ARE NOBLE, THEY ADMIRE INDIAN PHILOSOPHIES, ESPECIALLY IF THEY ARE PRESENTED BY CHARMING, MAGNETIC PERSONALITIES IN A FORCEFUL MANNER, BUT THEY ARE TOO BUSY TO ENQUIRE INTO THE SUBTLETIES OF THESE PERSONALITIES. AND THE INDIAN PEOPLE, RULED AND SUPPRESSED BY A FOREIGN NATION, AND NOT KNOWING THE TRUTH ABOUT THESE PREACHERS OF PHILOSOPHY FROM A DISTANCE, GETS A COMPENSATORY SATISFACTION WHEN MEMBERS OF ANOTHER FOREIGN NATION LEND EVEN HALF AN EAR TO THEIR PHILOSOPHY AND IMPART IT AS MUCH AS A FAINT SHADOW OF RECOGNITION.

SOMEONE MAY INQUIRE, AREN'T THESE PEOPLE DOING SOME GOOD? YES, BUT THAT DEPENDS UPON THE QUESTIONER'S VIEWPOINT, AND UPON WHETHER OR NOT HE LIKES TO SEE CULTURAL VALUES DELIBERATELY MANGLED BY THEM IN THE PROCESS. IN THE NAME OF INDIAN TEACHINGS, IN THE NAME OF FOUNDING BIG ORGANIZATIONS FOR THE GLORY OF THE HINDU RACE AND ADAPTING INDIAN PHILOSOPHY TO AMERICAN LIFE (WHICH SOME OF THESE TEACHERS VAUNT AS THEIR CHIEF MOTIVES IN LIFE) INDIAN PHILOSOPHY IS CERTAINLY VULGARIZED AND DRAGGED IN THE MUD.

FROM TAGORE TO A CERTAIN SWAMI WAS AN EXCRUCIATING CONTRAST AND DISAPPOINTMENT TO THOSE AMERICANS WHO HAVE HEARD AND KNOWN BOTH. THEIR SOULS SANK, SO THEY REMAINED SILENT. TAGORE THROUGH HIS WRITING AND HIS PERSONALITY, THROUGH HIS PHILOSOPHIC AESTHETICISM AND LYRICAL EXPRESSION, THROUGH HIS QUIET INDEPENDENCE, BROAD VISION AND DEEP HUMANITY HAS BEEN ENSHRINED IN THE HEARTS OF LOVERS OF LETTERS AND SEEKERS OF FREEDOM. HIS BOOKS HAVE BEEN AN INSPIRATION TO THOUSANDS AND THOUSANDS OF THOSE WHO ARE LOOKING FOR A NON-SECTARIAN PHILOSOPHY OF LIFE. THERE MAY BE ASSUMPTIONS IN IT WITH WHICH THE WESTERNERS MAY NOT BE FAMILIAR, BUT ITS SUBLIMITY AND DELICATE BEAUTY HAVE LIFTED THEM HIGH FROM THE COMMONPLACE. TAGORE WOULD NOT MAKE ANY CONCESSION TO THE JANGLING OF THE AMERICAN PRAGMATIC INSTINCT OF THE STREET. SO A POWERFUL SWAMI HAD TO

DO IT AND GIVE A HIGH FINISH TO THE JOB." ["ADVENTURES OF INDIAN PHILOSOPHY IN AMERICA," PUBLISHED IN THE MODERN REVIEW (CALCUTTA) IN FEBRUARY 1936 (PP. 165-69). [EXCERPTED]]

Here is the Los Angeles Times August 23, 1935 account:

"IN INDIA THOSE WHO KNEW SWAMI YOGANANDA AND SWAMI GIRI-DHIRANANDA, KNEW THEM AS COLLEGE CHUMS, BUT IN THE UNITED STATES SWAMI YOGANANDA CONVEYED THE IMPRESSION THAT HE WAS THE PRECEPTOR AND GIRI-DHIRANANDA WAS BUT HIS DISCIPLE. SWAMI GIRI-DHIRANANDA, WHO NOW IS KNOWN AS DR. BASU KUMAR BAGCHI, HINDU SCHOLAR AND PHILOSOPHER, TOLD SUPERIOR JUDGE WILLIS YESTERDAY THIS IMPRESSION THAT HIS FORMER FRIEND CREATED FOR HIM ON HIS COMING TO AMERICA WAS QUITE EMBARRASSING.

"SEEKING TO COLLECT $7900 FROM YOGANANDA, ASSERTEDLY DUE HIM ON A PROMISSORY NOTE SIGNED SIX YEARS AGO, DR. BAGCHI TESTIFIED AT LENGTH YESTERDAY SO THAT THE JUDGE MIGHT HAVE THE COMPLETE BACKGROUND OF THE TWO PERSONALITIES IN DETERMINING THE VALIDITY OF THE CLAIM.

"'IN THE SCHOOL AT RANCHI ESTABLISHED BY THE MAHARAJA OF KASIMBAZAR, WE WERE BOTH TEACHERS,' DR. BAGCHI TESTIFIED. 'WE WERE FRIENDS AND THEN YOGANANDA WENT TO AMERICA IN 1920. HE WROTE ME URGING ME TO FOLLOW HIM AND HELP HIM CARRY ON HIS WORK AND FINALLY AFTER HE SENT ME PASSAGE MONEY I CONSENTED.'

"'BUT I FOUND A DISGUSTING SITUATION,' DR. BAGCHI CONTINUED. 'HE HAD GIVEN PEOPLE THE IMPRESSION THAT I WAS AS A FOUNDLING, A PUNY LITTLE BOY THAT HE MIGHT HAVE FOUND IN THE GUTTER. HE WAS MY PRECEPTOR HERE, ALTHOUGH IN INDIA I HELD HIGHER SCHOLASTIC DEGREES AND RECEIVED HIGHER SALARIES.'"

In fact *Shastri Mahasaya* [*Swami Kebalananda*] was Dhiranandaji's *Kriya* initiation *guru*; about Yogananda's position as his *sannyas guru* in India, Dr. Bagchi later testified:

"DR. BAGCHI, HOWEVER, PREVIOUSLY TESTIFIED THAT HE WAS GIVEN SWAMISHIP BY YOGANANDA UNDER "RIDICULOUS AND FARCICAL" CIRCUMSTANCES AND THAT ON ONE OCCASION HE AGREED TO BE FRIENDS WITH YOGANANDA ONLY AFTER THE LATTER PROMISED NOT TO CONSIDER HIMSELF A "GURU" TO HIM (DR. BAGCHI)." (NEWS ACCOUNT IN AN OTHERWISE UNIDENTIFIED "EXPRESS," NEWSPAPER, AUGUST 28, 1935; SEE APPENDIX REFERENCE #6 FOR PHOTOCOPY OF ARTICLE)

In a June-9-1935 letter to Fiona Darling (Durga Ma), Yogananda instructs her to start an *ad hominem* offensive:

SHOW IMMIGRATION AUTHORITIES S.D.'S PUBLICITY FROM IOWA ABOUT ALIENATION OF AFFECTION SUIT. TELL IMMIGRATION THAT S.D. CAME AS A CELEBATE [SIC] PRIEST HE HAS GIVE UP [SIC] HIS PROFESSION AND CHURCH AND GOTTEN MARRIED AND HE IS NO LONGER A RELIGIOUS TEACHER. HE IS CROOKED AND EVIL AND AN UNDESIRABLE ALIEN AND MUST BE IMMEDIATELY SENT OUT. HIS STATUS IS CHANGED. [T]TAKE THIS ACTION IMMEDIATELY WITH IMMIGRATION. FILE FORGERY SUIT AGAINST S.D. FOR SIGNING MY NAME.

Dhirananda finally loses his spiritual idealism, as he testifies in court:

DR. BAGCHI . . . DECLARES HE RENOUNCED SWAMISHIP BECAUSE OF "MEDIEVAL SUPERSTITIONS CONNECTED WITH IT," (IBID.)

But Dhiranandaji (now in 1935 Basu Kumar Bagchi, Ph.D. candidate, University of Iowa) hasn't really "spilled the beans" on his childhood friend. He says nothing about finding Yogananda living with his disciple Laurie Pratt, nor does he publicly accuse him of fathering her child Moana.

He never does. And when the case went to court, all of Bagchi's claims were upheld, and all of Yogananda's counter-claims were declared false.

These false claims included:

1. If Yogananda would make Bagchi a Swami, he'd work for free for Yogananda.
2. That Bagchi threatened false publicity, if Yogananda did not sign the promissory note.
3. That Bagchi would falsely claim to be an associate and partner of Yogananda in the production of *The Science of Religion*, and various Yogoda booklets.
4. That Bagchi had stolen or misappropriated money from Yogananda.
5. That Bagchi got Yogananda to sign the promissory note by "threats, duress, menace or coercion."

Number 4 falsehood is poignant from a historical point of view. Dhirananda had punctiliously kept records, including a diary; but he couldn't produce them; Yogananda accused him in the counter-suit of theft of several thousands of dollars. Both men left for India, Yogananda before trial, and Dhirananda apparently during the trial. A hapless janitor found all the financial papers in the basement at Mother Center, and they were delivered to the Court.

That Yogananda had Dhirananda's diary is shown in his instructions to Durga Ma to (mis)quote from it to demonstrate that Dhirananda was greedy and calculating.

Did Virginia Wright follow this tactic when SRF, Inc. sued Ananda over copyright infringement? Plaintiff attorney Jon Parsons discusses Virginia's role in denying then admitting 1) that there is a second Yogananda will, and 2) they had found in the basement vault a second will signed by Yogananda in 1936 while still in India:

"IN THE SADNESS AND CEREMONY OF YOGANANDA'S SUDDEN PASSING, THERE WAS NO MENTION OF ANY WILL. AS THE HEIRS GRIEVED AND SRF GRABBED YOGANANDA'S MANTLE, NO ONE MENTIONED ANY WILL. BUT YOGANANDA HAD LEFT A WILL. HE HAD LEFT TWO WILLS. ONE HAD BEEN SIGNED IN 1935 BEFORE HE LEFT FOR INDIA, AND A SECOND IN 1936 WHILE HE WAS BACK IN CALCUTTA. DURING THE LAWSUIT SRF FIRST DENIED THERE WAS ANY WILL, BUT EVENTUALLY HAD TO PRODUCE BOTH OF THEM, AND THEN EXPLAIN WHY THEY HAD NOT BEEN DISCLOSED SOONER. UNFORTUNATELY, SRF WAS NEVER CALLED TO TASK BY YOGANANDA'S HEIRS WHO MIGHT HAVE BEEN DENIED THEIR RIGHTS GRANTED UNDER THOSE WILLS.

"SRF CLAIMED THAT YOGANANDA GAVE IT EVERYTHING HE OWNED, LOCK, STOCK AND BARREL, DURING HIS LIFETIME. THEREFORE, AS SRF FIRST EXPLAINED, THERE WAS NO WILL BECAUSE THERE WAS NO NEED FOR ONE. "WHY WOULD YOGANANDA NEED A WILL?" DAYA MATA ONCE ASKED. BUT WHEN THE WILLS TURNED UP, THEY SHOWED THAT YOGANANDA HAD CAREFULLY CONSIDERED WHICH ORGANIZATIONS WERE TO RECEIVE WHAT PORTION OF HIS ESTATE, AND SRF WAS NOT THE SOLE OBJECT OF HIS AFFECTION. DAYA AND ANANDA MATA DID THEIR BEST TO FORGET ABOUT THE WILLS. IT WAS ONLY AFTER LOSING A KEY MOTION, WHEN FURTHER SILENCE RISKED GREATER LOSS, THAT ANANDA MATA ALLEGEDLY STUMBLED ACROSS THE FIRST WILL IN THE BASEMENT VAULT. SHE AND HER SISTER HAD BOTH BEEN CLOSE TO YOGANANDA AT THE TIME THE WILLS WERE MADE, AND MUST HAVE KNOWN ABOUT THEM. BUT ANANDA MATA BLUSTERED ABOUT HER SHOCK AND SURPRISE TO NOW DISCOVER SUCH AN IMPORTANT DOCUMENT. WHEN WEEKS LATER SRF'S GROWING NEED PRECIPITATED ANANDA MATA'S DISCOVERY OF A SECOND FORGOTTEN WILL, HER CREDIBILITY TOOK FURTHER LUMPS. GOOD THINGS COME IN THREES, AND I HAVE ALWAYS WONDERED WHAT A THOROUGH SEARCH OF THE VAULT WOULD REVEAL." (A FIGHT FOR RELIGIOUS FREEDOM, CRYSTAL CLARITY PUBLISHER, 2012, JON PARSONS, AUTHOR)

Parsons describes how Virginia Wright's courtroom behavior affected Federal Judge Edward J. Garcia.

" . . . ANANDA MATA'S DISSEMBLING IN HER DECLARATIONS SO BADLY DAMAGED HER CREDIBILITY THAT GARCIA MADE A BIG DEAL ABOUT REFUSING TO CONSIDER WHAT SHE SAID IN HER DECLARATIONS. THE WILLS WERE EXTENSIVELY DISCUSSED IN THE FIRST APPEAL, AND I CAN TALK ABOUT THEM NOW ONLY BECAUSE THE COURT MADE THEM PUBLIC DURING THE APPEALS PROCESS . "

Who knows if SRF, Inc. were following a pattern set by Yogananda? Nonetheless even with the Judge's decision in favor of Bagchi Yogananda continued to defame him as a 'Judas.'

In later letters (published by Durga Ma) Yogananda wrote to James J Lynn

"AUGUST 22, 1945 – Even Jesus had his Judas, and my humble self had his Judases in Dhirananda and Nerode." (P. 164, A PARAMHANSA YOGANANDA TRILOGY OF DIVINE LOVE)

Apparently Durga Ma bought "the party line" given by Yogananda and (10 years later) repeats as true the falsehood pointed out in court by the presiding Judge and pointed out in the Los Angeles newspapers by Dr. Bagchi:

Master bore a deep love for DHIRANANDA, a disciple he had trained in India and brought to this country to help him with his SRF work in America. . . (P. 162, A PARAMHANSA YOGANANDA TRILOGY OF DIVINE LOVE; EMPHASIS ADDED)

To this day I fail to see Yogananda's justification for denouncing Dhirananda as a Judas, other than keeping the spotlight off himself regarding Laurie Pratt.

Swami Satyanandaji reflects on Yogananda's ability to bring unwitting curses upon people:

IT HAS BEEN SEEN SOMETIMES - WHILE TRYING TO SCOLD SOMEONE BECAUSE OF WRONGDOING - THAT [YOGANANDA] ENDED UP SAYING THINGS IN SUCH A WAY FROM THE HURT WITHIN HIM - THAT THOSE THINGS CAME TO FRUITION ALMOST LIKE A CURSE. HE ALSO WAS VERY SADDENED BY SEEING THE DESTRUCTION THAT THE POWER OF HIS OWN WORDS COULD CAUSE AS WELL. I CANNOT SAY THAT EVERYTHING HE SAID CAME TO FRUITION IN THIS WAY EVERY TIME EITHER. HOWEVER, BECAUSE OF THE CONFIRMATION OF THE POWER OF HIS WILL, I ALWAYS BELIEVED IN IT DEEPLY. YOGA NIKETAN. SWAMI SATYANANDA GIRI, A COLLECTION OF BIOGRAPHIES OF 4 KRIYA YOGA GURUS (KINDLE LOCATIONS 2517-2520, AD PASSIM). YOGA NIKETAN, INC., KINDLE EDITION.

Yogananda expressed the opinion that Dhiranandaji would not find God except thru Yogananda. This "curse" apparently didn't work. If you read Dr. Bagchi's family's accounts of him meditating in the basement at home while the children played around, over, and on his meditating posture, Basu Kumar's Samadhi achievement is illustrated. Not here the rebuking tone of Sriyukteswar,

"SIR, I AM MEDITATING," I [YOGANANDA] SHOUTED PROTESTINGLY. "I KNOW HOW YOU ARE MEDITATING," MY GURU CALLED OUT, "WITH YOUR MIND DISTRIBUTED LIKE LEAVES IN A STORM." YOGANANDA, PARAMHANSA. AUTOBIOGRAPHY OF A YOGI (REPRINT OF ORIGINAL 1946 EDITION) (P. 93). CRYSTAL CLARITY PUBLISHERS - A.KINDLE EDITION.

Swami Satyeswarananda confirms it,

"HE PRACTICED KRIYA TO THE LAST DAY OF HIS LIFE. HIS GRANDDAUGHTER (SYLVIA'S DAUGHTER), WENDY, NARRATED HER EXPERIENCE SAYING, "WHEN KUMAR [SHE USED TO CALL HER GRANDFATHER, KUMAR] SAT FOR MEDITATION, AFTER ABOUT FORTY-FIVE MINUTES, HE USED TO LOSE HIS EXTERNAL AWARENESS IN SUCH A WAY THAT IF SOMEONE SAT ON HIS THIGH OR ON HIS SHOULDER HE DID NOT KNOW OR WAS NOT AWARE AT ALL." (Mahamuni Babaji and His Legacy p. 965)

Appendix Reference #16 is an astounding picture in which Dhiranandaji's presence is airbrushed away!

Ironically before 1929 (when Dhiranandaji split-up with Yogananda) Dhirananda had already become friends with Eva Gladys Webber, Agnes Spencer (later Srimati Nerode), and Nirad Chowdhury (later Sri Nerode) (perhaps as early as 1926 at Mother Center). He did share with these three people what he knew about Yogananda and his penchant for sexual misbehavior. And the future Srimati Nerode writes of her eye witnessing Yogananda's sexual misbehavior and of the many girls that she and her husband transported surreptitiously away from Mother Center to "get away from the clutches of Swami Yogananda." (See Appendix Reference #4, "The Third Bettelu Letter" as well as #19and #20, Srimati's "Memoirs" and "Interview)"

The marriage of Gladys and Basu Kumar several years later at the home of Laurel Elizabeth Keyes is mentioned above.

Sri Nerode (Nirad Ranjan Choudhuri)

The sixth issue of the 1925-26 inaugural East-West magazine has on p. 31 the following announcement from the Detroit News about Sri Nerode:

"DETROIT NEWS

"BRAHMACHARI NERODE, A YOUNG BENGALI HINDU, HAS RECENTLY BEEN APPOINTED BY SWAMI YOGANANDA TO TAKE CHARGE OF THE DETROIT YOGODA CENTER. HE HAS BEEN INITIATED BY THE SWAMI AS A BRAHMACHARIN (WHICH MEANS, "ONE WHO IS SELF-DISCIPLINED") AND FROM THAT PREPARATORY ORDER HE MAY LATER BECOME A SWAMI. AFTER COMPLETING HIS TRAINING AS A BRAHMACHARIN AS PRESCRIBED BY HIS PRECEPTOR, HE MAY ELECT TO RETURN TO THE WORLD, OR DEVOTE THE REST OF HIS LIFE AS A SWAMI TO GOD'S WORK.

Sri Nerode had graduated from Harvard University in 1926, and his given name is Nirad Ranjan Choudhuri. I have seen "Nirad" and "Choudhuri" spelled different ways. I prefer the linguistic purity I find in the preciseness of Swami Satyeswaranandaji's scholarship. (Mahamuni Babaji and His Legacy, p. 965) The Detroit News is quoted in the 1927 Jan-April Volume II of East-West Nos. 2-3

"Brahmacharee Nerode, leader of the Detroit Yogoda Center, is a post-graduate of Calcutta, California and Harvard Universities. He is well versed in the Bible and in Vedanta, Upanishads, Gita and other Hindu scriptures, and is also a deep student of sociology and economics."

In the next issue (#4) of East-West (May-June 1927, p. 27) Sri Nerode continues to be presented by Yogananda's Yogoda outfit as Yogananda's disciple,

"Brahmacharee Nerode who comes here [Cincinnati, Ohio) once a month to keep alive the flame of Swami YOGANANDA'S teachings, is one of the latter's pupils, and is in charge of the very flourishing Detroit Center, where Swami Yogananda will spend some time."

I asked Dr. Anil Nerode (eldest child of the Nerodes) about the implication in these East-West articles that Yogananda had become Nerode's guru.

He denied it, and gives the following information about his father's family history:

"[THE] FAMILY MAINTAINED FOR HUNDREDS OF YEARS AN ASHRAM NEAR DELHI WHEN IT WAS THE CAPITAL OF THE MUGHAL EMPIRE. (1526-1857). THEY WORKED AS SCRIBES FOR THAT REGIME. WHEN THE EMPIRE FELL TO THE BRITISH, THE WHOLE FAMILY (80 OR MORE IN NUMBER) MOVED TO PARAIKORA NEAR CHITTAGONG WHICH WAS NEAR THE NEW CAPITAL CALCUTTA, SET UP THE ASHRAM SADHANA KUTIR AGAIN, AND EVENTUALLY LEARNED ENGLISH AND WORKED FOR THE BRITISH. SRI

Nerode was a disciple there of his famous Yogi grandfather Govindra Chandra Roy and his uncle Prasanna Kumar Roy. They were strongly involved with Ramakrishna." [FB post dated Dec. 30, 2017]

Satyeswaranandaji gives further detail of Nerode's interaction with Yoganandaji:

"**Nirad Ranjan Choudhuri** (September 11, 1887 - 1979)

"Nirad Ranjan Choudhuri was born on September 11, 1887 at Paraikora, Chattagram, currently Bangladesh, in a Brahmana family.

"From childhood he was very meritorious, and a very good student. While growing up he became an ideal person, patriotic, and a follower of Mahatma Gandhi (Mohandas Karam Chanda Gandhi).

"He was educated and was a Sanskrit scholar. He was very much interested in community service and was a local leader in his community. He was principal of a high school.

"In 1919, he left the post of high school principal and headed to the United States of America because of his involvement with Mahatma Gandhi.

"In the United States he joined Harvard University to study and received a graduate degree. His great inspiration was to introduce the ancient Yoga system in the service of American people.

In 1926, he joined with Yogananda in this noble cause. To describe Nirad Babu better in few a words we are going to quote from Yogananda who once reintroduced (because once they had broken their working relationship) Nirad (Nerode) to his followers.

""This is to inform you that Sri Nerode [Nirad] has been a real metaphysical teacher of Self-Realization - due to his many asserting spiritual qualities. The heart being one of the important seats of God - Sri Nerode has spiritual heart qualities - which has made his life alter [sic] of the Supreme Being. Sri Nerode's self-sacrificing qualities, unselfishness and Self-Realization of truth make him a rare teacher." — Swami Yogananda, President, S.R.F. Nov. 10, 1937" (Mahamuni Babaji, p. 982)

I found an undated letter from Yogananda to Nerode (with November 17th on it) expressing approval of Nerode's being called "Sri" rather than *brahmachari* and forgiving Nerode for the unspecified offense intimated by Satyeswaranandaji above:

"Dear Nerode, I am glad you at last agreed upon your name. Yes, Sri Nerode is alright & Srimati Nerode. Of course I have not only forgiven but forgotten even if there was any difference or adjustments. Between people who understand, there are periods of mental adjustments. True friends like good wine improve with age & adjustment periods." (See Appendix Reference "Yogananda accepts Sri Nerode's decision to go by the name 'Sri' rather than Brahmachari")

On the back of a letter from Ranendra Kumar Das to Srimati Nerode (not date but addressed from Indianapolis) Yogananda writes a Jan 6 1937 letter of apology with words similar to those quoted above to her husband from Yogananda. I have placed a copy of Yogananda's handwritten note. Again I do not know for what he is apologizing. (See #25, Yogananda's Jan 6 1937 Happy New Year Letter of Apology to Srimati Nerode)

Satyeswarananda discusses the history of Nerode's marriage and subsequent change of name to 'Sri':

"IN 1931, AFTER SOME YEARS, THEN BRAHMACHARI NERODE MARRIED A MORMON AMERICAN LADY, MISS AGNES SPENCER (AUGUST 9, 1907 - DECEMBER 4, 2002). THEIR MARRIAGE WAS FORMALLY SOLEMNIZED AND PRESIDED OVER BY YOGANANDA HIMSELF IN HIS MT. WASHINGTON CENTER AS A "YOGODA MARRIAGE" AND THE ANNOUNCEMENT WAS RUN IN THE LOCAL NEWSPAPER, ASSOCIATED PRESS, L. A. TIMES AND THE BOMBAY CHRONICLE, APRIL 26, 1931.(MAHAMUNI BABAJI, P. 985)

". . . AFTER THE MARRIAGE NIRAD DID NOT WANT TO USE THE TITLE BRAHMACHARI BUT YOGANANDA INSISTED (FOR PUBLIC RELATION PURPOSES FOR TEACHING). NIRAD, BEING AN HONEST GENTLEMAN, DID NOT ACCEPT IT. SO YOGANANDA PROPOSED A COMPROMISE FORMULA FOR HIM SIMPLY TO USE SRI NERODE. SINCE THEN HE WAS KNOWN AS SRI NERODE.

IN 1932, WHILE LIVING AND MANAGING THE MT. WASHINGTON CENTER, SRI NERODE'S FIRST SON, ANIL ROY SPENCER CHOUDHURY WAS BORN ON JUNE 4. THE FAMILY LIVED FOR SOME YEARS IN THE CENTER." (IBID, P. 986)

The marriage was in New Mexico because California law did not allow an 'alien' and an American citizen to marriage. They went to Arizona with a chaperone, but the white official there refused to do it. Here's a picture of the married couple in the snows of New Mexico:

Yes, Agnes (later dubbed 'Srimati' by Yogananda) lost her American citizenship. This is curious to me, since two other white American women married Indians. Dr. Sudhindra Bose married Anne Z. Bose, professor at Lindenwood College, Missouri; and of course Dr. Basukumar Bagchi married Eva Gladys Webber. I do not know, if those two ladies lost their American citizenship. Srimati became a naturalized American citizen sometime after their separation from the Self-Realization Fellowship work.

Pictured are Dr. and Mrs. Sudhindra Bose and also Dr. Bagchi, wife Eva Gladys and their two children:

If you read Srimati Nerode's interview and memoirs you will see how her husband's suggestion of gaining money for the organization was well received by Yogananda; one of those ways was to rent out rooms at Mother Center. One advertisement put out by Orpha L. Sahly (Director of Center Activities for Self-Realization Fellowship) posted a $40.00 per month rental that included "meals, light, heat, linen, and telephone service." (See Appendix Reference #26, "Sister Sahly Rental Announcement)

I do not know where Satyeswaranandaji got the idea that the rental was $500.00 per month. (p.987, Op. cit.)

The idea, however, cost the Nerodes their own rooms, and they wound up in the basement of Mother Center. Srimati observes in her memoirs how they subsisted on 17 cents a day. Anil became quite ill; at the pediatrician's urging she fed him bacon and other meat products because of his otherwise malnourished condition. Agnes reflects on the hardship caused by Yogananda's frequest visits to their room, eating the meats on the table or from the refrigerator, and leaving none for Anil, thus aggravating his malnutrition. Agnes asked her husband many times to leave Yogananda and the Yogoda work; she reflects on his loyalty. She then details the machinations of Yogananda and of the Wright sisters in driving them away from Yogoda. I mention this because after they left Yogoda, Sri Nerode was immediately denounced by Yogananda as a Judas. (See #19 and #20, Appendix Reference)

Early in 1938 Sri Nerode had received two handwritten letters from a Mother Center resident, Bettelu. Srimati details how Yogananda had gone to this girl and her mother's apartment in Hollywood and talked them into moving into Mother Center to live 'free of charge.'

Bettelu writes a letter to Sri Nerode detailing Yogananda's sexual behavior towards her; and starts by saying "Something has gone wrong in this organization;" and finishes 8 pages later hoping that Sri Nerode can do something that will keep other souls like her from being disillusioned. (Ibid., #2-4)

Yogananda had sworn her to secrecy; he would lock his bedroom door behind her and make her lay down on the floor next to his bed. After he was through with her (or perhaps after several hours of her continually repulsing his attempts at kissing, fondling her, or trying to penetrate her), he would call for Faye Wright to come to his room and walk Bettelu back to her own room. These things happened at both Mouth Washington and at Encinitas.

However she doesn't put in writing to Sri Nerode the worst of it; she found it more appropriate to tell another woman (Nerode's wife, Srimati) that Yogananda had mounted her clothed body one night, and refusing his attempts to penetrate her, he masturbated onto her clothing. (*Ibid.*)

She hadn't given Nerode the first letter, waiting a week instead, and then when Yogananda demanded a letter of character reference she gave Nerode the letter along with her second letter. She explains she's giving these two written accounts because now "I GAVE HIM THE TESTIMONY OF GOOD CHARACTER BECAUSE HE SAID IF I DID NOT HE WOULD HAVE YOU THROWN OUT IN THREE DAYS."

Srimati recounts how she and Nerode used their car to transport quite a few girls off Mount Washington surreptitiously to get them from   "the clutches of Swami" Here is an excerpt from Bettelu's mother 28 years later:

July 3-1966

Dear friends - the Nerodes - Betty and I always feel so happy when we hear from you - we believe you to be our true friends - you proved that when you helped us to get out of Swami's clutches.

All three 'Bettelu' letters are handwritten: two by Bettelu (in 1938) and one by her mother (1966).

Agnes Nerode describes how they were thrown out of SRF, Inc. Some of it is difficult to accept because of the patina of holiness that continues to surround Yogananda to this day.

Nerode himself tried many times to salvage the situation by urging Yogananda to marry. Yogananda became enraged every time Sri Nerode did so. Yogananda had objected to Nerode's marrying because "fewer women would come to hear him."

"AT ONE POINT, SRIMATI REFERRED TO WHAT WAS "COMMONLY KNOWN AS SWAMI'S HAREM". I ASKED HER TO ELABORATE ON "COMMONLY KNOWN". SHE REPLIED SRI, KHA- GEN, SRI DAS. SHE SAID THAT IN ARGUMENTS WITH SRI [NERODE, SRIMATI'S HUSBAND] THAT YOGANANDA HAD NEVER SAID HE WANTED TO REMAIN UNMARRIED BECAUSE HE FELT CELIBACY WAS IMPORTANT, BUT BECAUSE HE WAS AFRAID THAT HE WOULD NOT BE ATTRACTIVE TO HIS WOMEN FOLLOWERS. SRIMATI EXPLAINED THAT AT THAT TIME IN HOLLYWOOD, THE PRIVATE LIFE OF THE HOLLYWOOD ACTOR AND ACTRESSES WAS KEPT SECRET. FOR THE SAME REASON, SY WANTED TO REMAIN

UNMARRIED SO HE WOULD RETAIN HIS ATTRACTIVENESS FOR WOMEN. HE VERY MUCH USED HIS SEX, THE MALE-FEMALE ATTRACTION WITH WOMEN IN A CONSCIOUS WAY. "YOGANANDA WAS AS AWARE OF A PRETTY GIRL AS ANYONE ELSE," SRIMATI TOLD ME ON SEVERAL OCCASIONS." (#20, APPENIX REFERENCE)

If Yogananda had married, would he have taken several wives? Don't dismiss this as speculation: most folk do not know that C. Richard Wright (older brother of Faye and Virginia Wright) arrived at Mother Center with his Mormon wife and his mother-in-law.

"**ARRIVAL OF WRIGHTS**. [YOGANANDA] HAD BEEN IN SALT LAKE CITY TO LECTURE. HE RETURNED TO LA A FEW DAYS LATER. WE SAW 2 CAR LOADS FULL OF PEOPLE BRING THEIR THINGS IN. MRS. WRIGHT, RICHARD, FAYE, VIRGINIA AND A YOUNGER BROTHER WERE ONE FAMILY. THE OTHER FAMILY WAS A MOTHER, TWO SONS AND A DAUGHTER WHO WAS MARRIED TO RICHARD." (#19, IBID.)

The question arises in my mind that when Richard decided 'of a sudden' to marry again after his trip to India with Yogananda (and especially without telling Yogananda) was he taking on another Mormon wife? It gets even murkier when you remember Yogananda's protest that if he'd known that Richard wanted to marry, he could have introduced him to his 'soul-mate' while still in India.

More about marriage and sex will be discussed in the next chapter, "The Seventh Life."

That Sri Nerode was very loyal to Yogananda is indicated, I think, in his attempts to get Yogananda to marry so as to have a legitimate forum for his sexual expressions. Of course, by today's standards this might even sound like he was enabling Yogananda; but no, Yogananda would not consider marriage or any other change of his behavior.

Yogananda would, by today's standards, be considered a sexual predator: swearing girls to secrecy (in the name of confidentiality or guru-disciple relationship), claiming "a spiritual man can touch a woman and it won't be in the physical plane," locking the door to his room to stop egress and ingress of these girls, locking the Mt. Washington gate so that no one could leave without his permission (and even leaving on foot was a daunting task since it was at least a one mile walk down that twisting and turning San Rafael Boulevard or any of the other roads;* demanding written character references, etc.)

*"[SRIMATI] SAID THAT THE GEOGRAPHY OF THE PLACE WAS SUCH THAT ONCE YOU GOT ON THE HILL, YOU COULDN'T GET OFF WITHOUT P[ARAMAHANSA] Y[OGANANDA]'S KNOWING ABOUT IT. . . . YOU HAD TO HAVE HIS PERMISSION TO LEAVE THE GROUNDS. EVERYONE DID. S[WAMI] Y[OGANANDA] KEPT UP WITH WHAT EVERYONE WAS DOING. IT WAS A FULL-TIME JOB . . . (MEMOIRS, OP. CIT.)

Apparently many girls had escaped, and apparently had told neighbors; here is the account of the older couple who warned Laurel Elizabeth Keyes.

"IN MY SEARCH FOR A TEACHER . . . I TRIED MANY CHURCHES AND LECTURERS. AMONG THOSE LISTED IN THE CHURCH SECTION OF THE SUNDAY PAPER WAS YOGANANDA. SERVICES WERE HELD AT MT. WASHINGTON WHICH WAS A LONG WAY FROM WHERE I LIVED BUT THE PACIFIC ELECTRIC TRAIN AND BUSES COULD TAKE ME ALMOST ANYWHERE I WISHED TO GO, IF PLENTY OF TIME WERE ALLOWED FOR TRANSFERS. FREQUENTLY A TRANSFER CAUSED ME TO WAIT FOR 15 MINUTES OR MORE AND IT WAS DURING SUCH A PERIOD ON MY FIRST VISIT THAT THE DIRECTION OF MY LIFE MAY HAVE BEEN CHANGED. SUCH LITTLE THINGS MAY CAUSE THE ENTIRE COURSE OF A LIFE TO BE DIVERTED. YET, THERE ARE NO ACCIDENTS, WE ARE TOLD. WE LOOK AT THE FACTS AND WONDER WHAT MIGHT HAVE HAPPENED HAD WE MADE ANOTHER CHOICE.

"IT WAS A HOT, SUNDAY MORNING. AN ELDERLY COUPLE WAS SEATED IN ROCKING CHAIRS ON THEIR PORCH, CLOSE TO THE BUS STOP WHERE I WAS STANDING. AFTER A SHORT TIME THE WOMAN CALLED DOWN TO ME, KINDLY, "YOUNG LADY, WOULDN'T YOU LIKE TO COME HERE AND WAIT IN THE SHADE? THE BUS WON'T BE ALONG FOR AT LEAST ANOTHER 20 MINUTES. YOU JUST MISSED ONE."

GRATEFULLY I WENT UP AND SAT ON THE TOP STEP OF THE PORCH. THE GENTLEMAN ASKED WHERE I WAS GOING AND I TOLD HIM, "TO HEAR SWAMI YOGANANDA."

"THE COUPLE EXCHANGED KNOWING GLANCES AND THEN THE WOMAN LEANED TOWARD ME AND SAID CONFIDINGLY, "I WOULDN'T GO UP THERE IF I WERE YOU. THINGS ARE SAID ABOUT WHAT GOES ON UP THERE. NICE GIRLS JUST DON'T GO THERE."

"I WAS SHAKEN BY THEIR COMMENT AND TRIED TO QUESTION THEM. THEY HAD NOTHING DEFINITE TO OFFER OTHER THAN, "STRANGE, MYSTERIOUS THINGS GO ON UP THERE. IT'S NOTHING A YOUNG GIRL LIKE YOU WOULD WANT TO GET INTO."

"THEY WERE SO CONVINCING THAT I DECIDED TO FIND OUT MORE ABOUT IT BEFORE I ATTENDED MEETINGS THERE. I TOOK A BUS BACK HOME.

"EVENTUALLY I DID HEAR YOGANANDA WHEN HE HELD MEETINGS IN A DOWNTOWN BUILDING. IT MIGHT HAVE BEEN THAT SHADOW OF APPREHENSION CAST BY THE ELDERLY COUPLE, BUT I WATCHED AND LISTENED WITH CIRCUMSPECTION. (SUNDIAL, I COUNT THE SUNNY HOURS, LAUREL ELIZABETH KEYES, 1981, GENTLE PUBLISHING PUBLICATIONS, DENVER, COLORADO; PP. 99-100)

None the less Inner Culture magazine, Volume IX, #5 (1937), p. 44 had already credited Sri Nerode with giving Kriya to thousands of American disciples; and he continued for decades after the demise of Yogananda to give spiritual counsel and techniques for increasing the quality of one's consciousness.

Sri Nerode finally decided to terminate his partnership with Yogananda. Yogananda publicly called him a 'dirty chiseler' and produced a statement apparently signed by Nerode that Nerode would work for Yogananda in exchange for board and room. (See 'The Dirty Chiseler' in Appendix Reference #27)

In this account Yogananda makes an astoundingly untruthful assertion:

"'CHOWDHURY HAD BEEN DRIVEN OUT OF THE FLOCK BECAUSE HE . . . VIOLATED OUR RULES. HE MARRIED A WHITE WOMAN, WHICH IS DIRECTLY FORBIDDEN IN OUR LAWS." (Ibid.)

By now the Nerodes have been married for approximately seven years. In that time Yogananda's East-West magazine consistently supported US Federal legislation that would have expanded the definition of 'white people' to include Indian Aryans and allow them to become US citizens. (p. 19, Nov-Dec., 1926, East-West, Volume II, No. 1; East-West, Vol II, 1926-1927, Sept-Oct, No. 6, p. 18); and nowhere in his Yogoda is there a prohibition against marrying white people. If Yogananda is going to insist on following laws, he couldn't, wouldn't, and shouldn't have performed the wedding of the Nerodes: as a swami he has no authority to do such a thing; and the 'walking around Mother Center' ceremony hardly qualifies for the traditional Hindu marriage rites.

Swami Satyeswarananda clarifies:

"YOGANANDA COMPLAINED THAT NERODE HAD MARRIED A "WHITE WOMAN" WHEN YOGANANDA HIMSELF HAD FORMALLY SOLEMNIZED AND PRESIDED OVER THEIR MARRIAGE IN HIS OWN ASRAM AND SET AN EXAMPLE OF YOGODA MARRIAGE. IT SHOULD BE MENTIONED HERE THAT IN THE VEDIC CULTURE A   RENUNCIATE SWAMI IS NOT EVEN SUPPOSED TO ATTEND A MARRIAGE CEREMONY NOT TO SPEAK OF PRESIDING OVER IT AND ACTING LIKE A PRIEST WHEN ONE EVEN DOES NOT EVEN HAVE THE SACRED THREAD)."

It is never been clear to me why Sri Nerode wanted Yogananda's marriage ceremony. Perhaps it is because Nerode held Yogananda in such high esteem.

As for Yogananda's assertion that "Chowdhury had been driven out of the flock . . ." read Srimati's detailed written account of Yogananda's "[leading] an entire group in the mornings around the Tennis Courts, the Garden, back and forth on the sidewalk chanting to excise the Nerodes." (Appendix Reference, # 20, Interview with Srimati)

This excision was on top of the attempted palace coup led by the Wright sisters, according to Srimati's memoirs.

"THE FROCKING

"AT A LIGHT TAPPING ON THE DOOR I ADMIT A YOUNG MAN OF ABOUT 18 YEARS. HE DARTED INSIDE AND QUICKLY CLOSED THE DOOR. BOY TOLD US THAT SWAMI YOGANANDA AND GIRLS GOT TO GET US AT TEMPLE. HE WAS NEW THERE. . . HE UNDERSTOOD TALKING ABOUT US BY OTHERS. TOLD US THAT SWAMI YOGANANDA WOULD ARREST [NERODE] OR THROW HIM OUT AT NEXT MEETING AT 17TH S[TREET] TEMPLE. I WAS TEMPERED. SRI COULD NOT BELIEVE, I DO.

"SWAMI YOGANANDA INNER CIRCLE NEVER WENT TO HEAR SRI NERODE AT 17TH ST. SUNDAY MORNING I DROVE TO 17TH S[TREET]. SAW MOUNT WASHINGTON CARS AND A STRANGE ONE IN FRONT WITH A MAN WHO DID NOT LOOK LIKE HE BELONGED THERE. SAW SWAMI YOGANANDA'S CROWD COME BACK. TOLD SRI NERODE AND DROVE OFF. I DID NOT LET SRI NERODE GO IN EVEN IF HE WANTED TO GO IN. I WASADAMANT.

"IT WAS JUST AS THE BOY HAD WARNED.

"THE WRIGHT'S (FAMILY DAYA MATA) WERE GOING TO DEFROCK SRI NERODE – TAKE HIS ROBE OFF IN FRONT OF CROWD AND THROW HIM OUT. THEY HAD A NEWSPAPER REPORTER IN FRONT TO SEE SRI NERODE THROWN OUT. IT WAS THE WRIGHTS LAST DITCH EFFORT TO GET RID OF SRI NERODE. THEY WANTED TO DISGRACE HIM SO HE COULD NO LONGER TEACH. ONE BROTHER, 2 SISTERS AND THE MOTHER WERE THERE. WE AVOIDED THAT SCENE. ALL BECAUSE OF THE GIRLS." ((IBID.)

That is the one truth Yogananda cited accurately: the Nerodes were 'driven out' of 'the flock.'

There is an interesting letter to share about Sri Nerode's character from the University of Kentucky where he was an instructor (even at the age of 85), and according to the writer, Dr. Harry Epstein, professor in the Department of English,

"TO WHOM IT MAY CONCERN:

"IF YOU ARE INTERESTED IN PROBLEMS OF MENTAL HEALTH AND PSYCHIC WELLBEING, EITHER FOR REASONS OF PERSONAL NEED OR GENERAL SOCIAL CONCERN, THEN YOU WILL BE INTERESTED IN THE WORK BEING DONE BY SRI NERODE. NERODE IS A YOGI, BUT HE IS NO INDIAN FAKIR DAZZLING HIS STUDENTS WITH MYSTICISM OR FOGGY MINDED SPIRITUALITY. YOU WILL FIND THAT HE IS A MAN OF HIGHEST RATIONALITY AND PRINCIPLE. HE LEFT MONEY IN INDIA WHERE HIS FAMILY WAS VERY WELL TO DO AND HAS BROKEN WITH A PROSPEROUS AMERICAN ORGANIZATION FOR REASONS OF CONSCIENCE. HE IS A GRADUATE OF THE UNIVERSITY OF CALCUTTA AND HAS DONE POST-GRADUATE WORK AT HARVARD AND BERKELEY. AT EIGHTY-FIVE HE IS STILL FILLED WITH ENERGY (HE CARRIES A TEACHING LOAD WHICH WOULD EXHAUST MOST OF MY COLLEAGUES HERE AT KENTUCKY) AND DISPLAYS A KEEN, LIVELY AND EXUBERANT MIND. HE EATS MEAT; HE HAS MARRIED AN AMERICAN WOMAN AND HAS THREE SONS WHOM HE HAS PUT THROUGH THE UNIVERSITY OF CHICAGO. THE

OLDEST OF HIS CHILDREN IS THE NOTED LOGICIAN, ANIL NERODE, WHO HAS BEEN INCLUDED IN THE MOST RECENT WHO'S WHO."

Consider "he carries a teaching load which would exhaust most of my colleagues here at Kentucky," and Dr. Epstein credits Sri Nerode with his assistance on his Ph.D. dissertation.

Rare and well-deserved praise indeed; consider the praise from the pen of the future Swami Premanandaji who acknowledges that the Yogoda work would have collapsed if it weren't for the Nerodes.

"ON HOW HAPPY I WAS TO SEE AND BE WITH YOU! YOU KNOW, NERODEJI, MY RESPECT FOR YOU IS MANY SIDED AND IMMENSE. I AM SO DELIGHTED TO REALISE HOW DEEPLY YOU FEEL THE WELFARE OF THE MOVEMENT FOR WHICH YOU HAVE SACRIFICED YOUR WHOLE LIFE; YES, FOR WHICH YOU WENT NAKED AND HUNGRY. YOU HAVE STOOD BY GURUDEVA WHEN ALL LEFT HIM. YOU GAVE YOUR BLOOD TO KEEP HIS WORK ALIVE. I AM FULLY AWARE OF ALL THIS. TO ME YOU HAVE ALWAYS BEEN AN INSPIRATION. I WISH I HAD THE SAME SPIRIT OF SACRIFICE AS YOU HAVE. YOU HAVE MY RESPECT, YES, MY DEVOTION TOO.

WELL, BAUDI [AFFECTIONATE TERM FOR SRIMATI], DO YOU WANT ME TO TELL YOU WHAT IMPRESSION YOU HAVE ON ME? YOU ARE A SAKTI, THE EMBODIMENT OF THE STRENGTH OF LOVE AND THE POWER OF SACRIFICE. FEW, FEW WILL EVER DO WHAT YOU HAVE DONE FOR GURU-DEVA. IF IT WERE NOT FOR YOUR POWERFUL SPIRIT THE WHOLE WORK WOULD HAVE BEEN MOST PROBABLY WIPED OUT. YOU HAVE SAVED THE WORK.

JUST THINK, YOU TWO IN TWO MOST CRITICAL OCCASIONS IN THE LIFE OF THE MOVEMENT HAVE BEEN THE SAVING POWER OF THE WHOLE WORK IN U. S. A., YES AND THEREBY IN INDIA TOO. I AM FULLY AWARE OF ALL THIS. (APPENDIX REFERENCE #29 JOTIN'S LETTER TO THE NERODES)

Read Srimati's account of Jotin's reaction when they told him of Yogananda's sexual behavior. (APPENDIX REFERENCE #'S 19 AND 20; ALSO READ JOTIN'S LETTER, IBID.)

One of the two things the Nerode's did that "saved the work," was to speak with JJ Lynn on at least two occasions encouraging him not to leave Yogananda due to his doubts about Yogananda. Srimati writes,

WE HAD MET LYNN WHEN WE WERE IN KANSAS CITY. HE OWNED A STRING OF CAFETERIAS AND AN INSURANCE COMPANY AND HAD A VERY IMPRESSIVE HOME IN A WEALTHY SECTION OF KANSAS CITY. HE HAD ASKED SRI ABOUT YOGANANDA AND SAID HE WAS NOT REALLY IMPRESSED WITH HIS SINCERITY AND MOTIVES. HE WAS NOT GOING TO FOLLOW HIM. SRI CONVINCED HIM YOGANANDA WAS OK. HE DECIDED TO STAY IN THE MOVEMENT AND PROMISED SRI THE MONEY TO BUILD A TEMPLE IN MIAMI. (OP. CIT., #19 SRIMATI'S MEMOIRS, P. 5)

After their departure Sister Gyanamata, who acknowledges in SRF, Inc.'s collection of her letters, *God Alone*, that many things about the monastic life she liked and many things disappointed her, but she finally came to the full vision of the guru-disciple relationship.

That being said, she of all people saw past her gurudeva's blustery hyperbole and saw the Nerodes for the saintly souls they are, for the contribution they had made and would continue to make.

In an April, 1936 letter to Srimati she says of her, her child Anil, and of Sri Nerode, that they are among those "of whom the world is not worthy." (Appendix Referenced #30)

Here is an excerpt from an otherwise undated letter from Sister Gyanamataji:

"WE WERE SO GLAD TO HAVE YOU WITH US, AND NOW YOU KNOW FOR YOURSELF JUST HOW EVERYTHING IS AND HOW THE WORK IS CARRIED ON. THINGS THAT COULD NOT BE EXPLAINED PROPERLY IN A LETTER. I LOOK BACK TO THE DAYS THAT YOU WERE HERE WITH DEEPER FEELING, THINK, THAN ANY OF THE OTHERS CAN HAVE. YOU WERE MY FIRST BEST FRIEND AT THE CENTER, AND I HAVE NEVER FORGOTTEN WHAT YOU DID FOR ME. ALSO YOU WERE THE FIRST TO EXPRESS THE WISH THAT I MIGHT LIVE HERE. SWAMIJI MAY HAVE FELT IT.

HE WROTE ME AFTER MR. BISSETT'S DEATH THAT HE HAD LONG KNOWN THAT THIS WAS TO BE MY HOME -- BUT YOU WERE THE FIRST TO TRY TO BRING IT ABOUT.

I HOPE THINGS ARE IMPROVING FOR YOU. THERE MUST BE A GREAT WORK FOR YOU TO DO, FOR YOU ARE A WONDERFUL TEACHER AND ALWAYS ESTABLISH A STRONG HOLD UPON THE AFFECTIONS OF YOUR STUDENTS." (APPENDIX REFERENCED #31)

What a promise of the future! "THERE MUST BE A GREAT WORK FOR YOU TO DO, FOR YOU ARE A WONDERFUL TEACHER AND ALWAYS ESTABLISH A STRONG HOLD UPON THE AFFECTIONS OF YOUR STUDENTS."

Dr. Epstein's letter is adequate demonstration of the high regard accorded Yogi Nerode.

Chapter 10. The Seventh Life

The Role of Suicide in the Spiritual Life

The term 'suicide' comes from two Latin words, sui and caedere; the many 'spinoffs' of meanings include self-control, taking charge, and (most commonly understood in the West) killing oneself.

But this discussion has to do with the deeper meaning suggested by the terms "self-control" or "taking charge."

"THE TERM "SUICIDE" COMES FROM THE TWO LATIN WORDS, SUI MEANING "SELF" AND CAEDERE MEANING "TO SEIZE, CONTROL, KILL." WHILE WE TRANSLATE IT AS KILLING ONESELF, THE ELEMENT OF CONTROL, OF CONTROLLING ONE'S LIFE OR CIRCUMSTANCES MUST NOT BE OVERLOOKED. IN THE SEVENTH OF EIGHT SKILLS THAT RUSSELL AND BEIGLE TEACH POLICE REGARDING RESPONSE TO A SUICIDAL PERSON, THEY POINT OUT THAT THE SUICIDAL PERSON IS IN CONTROL. "REMEMBER THAT THE PERSON ATTEMPTING SUICIDE IS IN CONTROL. ATTEMPTERS HAVE SEIZED ULTIMATE CONTROL OVER THEIR LIVES. . .YOUR JOB IS TO TAKE CONTROL FROM THESE PEOPLE IN AN UNOBTRUSIVE WAY BY SHOWING YOUR SINCERE DESIRE TO HELP THEM OUT OF THE SITUATION." (Russell, Harold E. and Allan Beigel. Understanding Human Behavior for Effective Police Work, p. 248; 3rd ed. New York: Basic Books, 1990.)

In the East there is a far wider understanding and tolerance for self-chosen behavior that results in death than there is in the West. One of the first customs that comes to mind is that of *suttee* (aka *sati*) in which an Indian widow throws herself on her husband's on cremation *pyre*. Yogananda has observed that Indian wives prefer to die before their husband so that they can be seen as 'dying in harness.'

But *suttee* can be utilized as a form of showing love and devotion by a wife whose husband dies first.

There are as well the acts of those God-hungry souls whose separation from the Divine cannot be tolerated any longer. Yogananda describes in *Autobiography of a Yogi*

""On another occasion Babaji's sacred circle was disturbed by the arrival of a stranger. He had climbed with astonishing skill to the nearly inaccessible ledge near the camp of the master.

"'Sir, you must be the great Babaji.' The man's face was lit with inexpressible reverence. 'For months I have pursued a ceaseless search for you among these forbidding crags. I implore you to accept me as a disciple.'

"When the great guru made no response, the man pointed to the rocky chasm at his feet.

"'If you refuse me, I will jump from this mountain. Life has no further value if I cannot win your guidance to the Divine.'

"'Jump then,' Babaji said unemotionally. 'I cannot accept you in your present state of development.'

"The man immediately hurled himself over the cliff. Babaji instructed the shocked disciples to fetch the stranger's body. When they returned with the mangled form, the master placed his divine hand on the dead man. Lo! he opened his eyes and prostrated himself humbly before the omnipotent one.

"'You are now ready for discipleship.' Babaji beamed lovingly on his resurrected chela. 'You have courageously passed a difficult test. Death shall not touch you again; now you are one of our immortal flock' . . ." (PARAMHANSA YOGANANDA. AUTOBIOGRAPHY OF A YOGI (REPRINT OF THE PHILOSOPHICAL LIBRARY 1946 FIRST EDITION) (P. 191). CRYSTAL CLARITY PUBLISHERS - A. KINDLE EDITION.)

Obviously this ardent devotee wasn't held to the law that says a successful suicide must pass through seven successive lifetimes each of which inevitably brings the offender back in the seventh life to face the same issues from which previously he had declined to learn any further lessons.

There is another similar case in Totapuri, the guru of Ramakrishna Paramhansa. During a case of severe diarrhea the saint experienced such pain he attempted suicide. Divine Mother did not criticize him, but elevated his vision.

St. Paul had learned such an effective way of daily stilling the natural tumult of respiration that he cried out to the church at Corinth,

"Verily, I protest by our rejoicing which I have in Christ, I die daily." (I Corinthians 15:31) (PARAMHANSA YOGANANDA. AUTOBIOGRAPHY OF A YOGI (REPRINT OF THE PHILOSOPHICAL LIBRARY 1946 FIRST EDITION) (P. 150). CRYSTAL CLARITY PUBLISHERS - A. KINDLE EDITION.)

Now that is a death worth dying! And certainly that is the natural outcome for all those who have by technique or divine grace found themselves transported beyond the senses into the living Presence of the Divine.

I have seen the manuscript of one wondrous Master who was so desirous of God, that even though he had mastered the yogic science of Samadhi, and even though he was blessed with the living guidance of a guru, still he threw himself off a mountain to accelerate the long awaited union. He says, as I recall my vision,

"WHEN I ROUSED FROM UNCONSCIOUSNESS, I FOUND MYSELF IN THE ARMS OF MY GURU."

Isn't that precious?! And the guru, understanding, introduced him to the Divine Union.

Venkataraman tells the story of one devotee who vowed death by suicide, if he couldn't achieve his desire. He tells of Tukaram whose poems the Brahmins claimed were not acceptable: they were not written in Sanskrit and a non-Brahmin could not write in that style of poetry. They challenged him that he should prove his acceptability to them by throwing his poetry into the river, and

"THAT IF HE WERE A TRUE DEVOTEE OF GOD, THE MANUSCRIPTS WOULD REAPPEAR. IT IS SAID THAT TUKARAM THEN COMMENCED A FAST-UNTO-DEATH, INVOKING THE NAME OF GOD. AND AFTER THIRTEEN DAYS OF HIS FAST, THE MANUSCRIPTS OF TUKARAM'S POEMS REAPPEARED. THIS MADE HIS DETRACTORS AS HIS FOLLOWERS AND HE ACQUIRED THE REPUTATION AS A SAINT, SANT TUKARAM." (M. VENKATARAMAN. GREAT SAINTS OF INDIA (P. 81). UNKNOWN. KINDLE EDITION.)

June McDaniel tells this story,

"WHEN TOTAPURI, A NAKED MENDICANT WITH MATTED HAIR, CAME TO DAKSINESWAR . . . HE HAD A VISION OF THE DIVINE MOTHER, WHICH LASTED THROUGH THE NIGHT AND MORNING, WHEN HE HAD AN ATTACK OF DYSENTERY SO SEVERE THAT HE ATTEMPTED SUICIDE. (THE MADNESS OF THE SAINTS: ECSTATIC RELIGION IN BENGAL, CHAPTER THREE, P. 98)

This story is all the more amazing because Totapuri was the instrument by which Ramakrishna Paramhansa was relieved of his delusion that the Divine Mother was a 'real' person, rather than the necessary fiction that we all use to move ourselves from one pinnacle of spiritual insight to higher pinnacles.

But the rest of us less spiritually developed souls who commit suicide are still bound by the law that requires an ineluctable round of seven rebirths until the soul is forced to come 'face to face' with the same issues previously avoided. Since we are all on the spiritual path, according to Yogananda, then there is no 'retardation' of spiritual growth, no 'hell to pay,' other than that the soul will have issues more clearly focused in his daily life than most souls.

In my case I found from earliest memory episodes of death by suicide. A parishioner of my preacher Dad's church shot herself. She lingered, rational and repentant, for several days in the hospital. I was allowed to speak with her, and we reminisced about all the animals she would feed in her isolated Oregon mountain cottage. My brother Paul and I used to hide in the nearby trees and watch as she fed birds, squirrels, deer (and especially the baby fawns!). It was magical for us. But as she and I talked at her hospital bedside, she mentioned how much she missed her recently deceased husband.

We avowed our loved for one another at that visit; and later that week she died.

Hers wasn't the only funeral of a suicide over which my Dad presided.

Then later in college I attempted, unsuccessfully, to kill myself after finding my philosophical and religious studies were "going nowhere." Finding myself still alive, I "dusted myself off" emotionally, and thirty minutes later attended a luncheon with one of my spiritual heroes, E. Stanley Jones, at Bresee Avenue Church of the Nazarene.

During my college career I was privileged to meet psychiatrist Dr. Viktor Frankl and to hear him talk of his experiences in the Auschwitz Concentration Camp. He spoke of choosing how he would survive the camp before he was ever captured and incarcerated there; he credited his decision to 'be of service to others' with keeping him sane, useful, and alive. He spoke of several inmates who committed suicide in their ordeal; he was nonjudgmental, and as I recall, he found that there was little he could do or say to someone who had already passed judgment on their 'terrible lot.'

Dr. Frankl refused to let his circumstances define him, and found that he and many others did well emotionally and mentally in that death-dealing camp while seeking to be of service to others.

I am now reminded of Laura Hillenbrand's book, *Unbroken: A World War II Story of Survival, Resilience, and Redemption.* In that story Louis Zamperini recounts his survival of incredible circumstances during the Pacific phase of WWII; he recounts to Laura the ineluctable fate of one of the three air plane crash survivors during the many days they spent floating in their raft hoping for rescue. One of the soldiers slipped into morose thinking of being doomed, and one day died in front of them, so to speak, because he had given up hope.

He was the only one of the three who didn't survive that experience on the raft.

In my transfer to UT-Austin to pursue doctoral study of Biblical Hebrew, I again ran into successful suicides, one of a coworker at the gas station where I worked pumping gas, and the other at the mental health clinic of the Austin-Travis County MHMR Center where I worked as an alcoholism counselor.

What intrigued me about successful suicides in Austin during my time with the mental health authority was that they were primarily committed by affluent people, hardly ever by those who were still struggling to "make ends meet."

During those years the US Government Office of Technology and the US Department of Labor used to keep statistical reports on suicides in the United States. I recount this in my 2003 textbook *Enhancing Police Response to Persons in Mental Health Crisis* (Charles C. Thomas, Publishers).

In-spite-of the emphasis on mental health causes of suicide, the truth continues that barely 50% of all suicides can be attributed to mental health. I raised the question in 2003 and I raise it here: what about those whose suicides are not attributable to mental health." Several years ago the Department of Labor published research showing that there was no correlation between occupation and suicide rate. Until then it was thought that there was a high correlation somewhat as follows: 1st – dentists, 2nd – police, 3rd – ministers, 4th – plumbers, etc." (*Op. cit.*, p. 99)

However in the law enforcement profession the 1996 documentary film, "Memphis PD: War on the Streets," claims [Memphis PD: War on the Streets, Home Box Office. DiPersio, Vince and William Guttentag, producers. 1996] "among police twice as many officers die every year by their own hand than die in the line of duty." (quoted in Enhancing Police Response, p. 99) I haven't any statistics for police or other professions suicide rates as of today's date.

Perhaps the thought of suicide is uppermost in mind even while engaging in enjoyable activities. The reality is that anyone anywhere anytime can commit suicide. In my career in mental health crisis intervention, one of the balances to push with a suicidal person was to remind them that they could always 'do it.' Their ambivalence about it is understandable; and by reminding them that there's 'no rush,' the suicidal person can obtain more time for themselves to consider other options. Even the 'great ones' like Yogiraj Lahiri Mahasaya can be ambivalent about death; Sriyukteswar tells the story,

""GURUDEVA, THE DIVINE MASTER ASKED ME TO GIVE YOU A MESSAGE. "TELL LAHIRI," HE SAID, "THAT THE STORED-UP POWER FOR THIS LIFE NOW RUNS LOW; IT IS NEARLY FINISHED."' "AT MY UTTERANCE OF THESE ENIGMATIC WORDS, LAHIRI MAHASAYA'S FIGURE TREMBLED AS THOUGH TOUCHED BY A LIGHTNING CURRENT. IN AN INSTANT EVERYTHING ABOUT HIM FELL SILENT; HIS SMILING COUNTENANCE TURNED INCREDIBLY STERN. LIKE A WOODEN STATUE, SOMBER AND IMMOVABLE IN ITS SEAT, HIS BODY BECAME COLORLESS. I WAS ALARMED AND BEWILDERED. NEVER IN MY LIFE HAD I SEEN THIS JOYOUS SOUL MANIFEST SUCH AWFUL GRAVITY. THE OTHER DISCIPLES PRESENT STARED APPREHENSIVELY. "THREE HOURS PASSED IN UTTER SILENCE. THEN LAHIRI MAHASAYA RESUMED HIS NATURAL, NATURAL, CHEERFUL DEMEANOR, AND SPOKE AFFECTIONATELY TO EACH OF THE CHELAS. EVERYONE SIGHED IN RELIEF. "I REALIZED BY MY MASTER'S REACTION THAT BABAJI'S MESSAGE HAD BEEN AN UNMISTAKABLE SIGNAL BY WHICH LAHIRI MAHASAYA UNDERSTOOD THAT HIS BODY WOULD SOON BE UNTENANTED. HIS AWESOME SILENCE PROVED THAT MY GURU HAD INSTANTLY CONTROLLED HIS BEING, CUT HIS LAST CORD OF ATTACHMENT TO THE MATERIAL WORLD, AND FLED TO HIS EVER-LIVING IDENTITY IN SPIRIT. BABAJI'S REMARK HAD BEEN HIS WAY OF SAYING: 'I SHALL BE EVER WITH YOU.'"   (PARAMHANSA YOGANANDA. AUTOBIOGRAPHY OF A YOGI (REPRINT OF THE PHILOSOPHICAL LIBRARY 1946 FIRST EDITION) (PP. 213-214). CRYSTAL CLARITY PUBLISHERS - A. KINDLE EDITION.)

". . . and fled to his ever-living identity in Spirit." O, that the rest of us mere mortals could attain such equanimity! But this life, this living is, for each of us, ours alone; not our community, neither nation, nor family, etc. Mary Emily Bradley writes poignantly of her death:

"IN DEATH"
HOW STILL THE ROOM IS! BUT A WHILE AGO
THE SOUND OF SOBBING VOICES VEXED MY EARS,
AND ON MY FACE THERE FELL A RAIN OF TEARS--
I SCARCE KNEW WHY OR WHENCE, BUT NOW I KNOW.
FOR THIS SWEET SPEAKING SILENCE, THIS SURCEASE
OF THE DUMB, DESPERATE STRUGGLE AFTER BREATH,
THIS PAINLESS CONSCIOUSNESS OF PERFECT PEACE,
WHICH FILLS THE PLACE OF ANGUISH -- IT IS DEATH!
WHAT FOLLY TO HAVE FEARED IT! NOT THE BEST
OF ALL WE KNEW OF LIFE CAN EQUAL THIS,
BLENDING IN ONE THE SENSE OF UTTER REST,
THE VIVID CERTAINTY OF BOUNDLESS BLISS!
O DEATH, THE LOVELINESS THAT IS IN THEE,
COULD THE WORLD KNOW, THE WORLD WOULD CEASE TO BE.

"Could the world know, the world would cease to be." Wow! And she meant it! Look how she castigates her loving husband's interference in her death:

""BUT OH! THAT YOU HAD MADE NO SIGN,
THAT I HAD HEARD NO CRYING!
FOR NOW THE YEARNING VOICE IS MINE,
AND THERE IS NO REPLYING:
DEATH NEVER COULD SO CRUEL BE
AS LIFE – AND YOU – HAVE PROVED TO ME!""

(*Beyond Recall*, quoted in my te

I love to listen to evangelist Uncle Buddy Robinson's tape recording of his visit to heaven. He describes the journey, the view, and unmatched beauty of the music rolling over the hills, and his visit with his beloved Jesus. Listen to it, if you can; I think so much about it that I republished the paperback a couple years ago, *My Hospital Experience*. (Publisher: CreateSpace Independent Publishing Platform; 1st edition (December 21, 2014 ; ISBN-10: 1505658276; ISBN-13: 978-1505658279).

Nonetheless Yogananda has clearly stated that death will not automatically promote you to sainthood. It is far easier to seek these higher states while living in your current situation. And that is one of the things I have learned in this seventh life; more importantly I have learned that even though one's most trusted spiritual guide should betray you, you must continue anyway trusting always in yourself, not waiting for the experts -- because ultimately all gurus, all so-called 'experts' must betray you through their death, their unavailability, their inability to think and decide for you, etc., etc.

I remember the story of the SRF nun at Mother Center who had been accidentally gassed by truck exhaust fumes. Yogananda did all he could for her, but she in her innervated state claimed it impossible to do anything for herself wthat he would suggest. Finally Yogananda acknowledged he couldn't (and therefore wouldn't) do anything more for her; she could make the effort herself, or die. She made the effort and recovered completely.

I also recall that Yogananda did not interfere in the suicide of his friend, Kodak camera inventor George Eastman.

That which I have learned through the living of these seven lives is found in the next section, 'when to say "no" to the guru.'

The real role of suicide in the spiritual life is capsulized in the lives of all great saints who are able to do as St. Paul and Yogiraj Lahiri Mahasaya did. In Sanskrit it's called 'Mahasamadhi,' the yogi's final conscious exit from the body. They do that when they receive the call from their beloved Lord; just as Jesus did on the cross.

When to Say "No" to the Guru

Sriyukteswar extracted the promise from Yogananda that Yogananda would rescue Sriyukteswar if he found him slipping from his exalted spiritual state. This is one of the times when it is necessary to say "no" to the guru. Do you remember the story of Krishna's feigning a headache and demanding that someone of the gopis around him should relieve it by standing on his head?! No one would relieve him of his headache for fear of hell fire, should they perform such a sacrilegious act. Radha, the chief female disciple of Krishna, heard of Krishna's anguished demand, and immediately she stepped on his head with her bare feet. The gopis were aghast at her act. But Krishna was immediately relieved of his anguish, and thanked Radha for her selfless act. Of course, she didn't go to hell, etc.

Venkataraman tells another story of saying "no" to the guru.

"THEN [THIRUKOTTIYUR] NAMBI DULY INITIATED RAMANUJA ON THE THIRUMANTRAM WITH A CONDITION. HE SAID, "RAMANUJA! KEEP THIS MANTRA A SECRET. THIS IS A POWERFUL ONE. THOSE WHO REPEAT THIS MANTRA WILL ATTAIN SALVATION. SO DO NOT GIVE IT TO EVERYBODY. GIVE IT ONLY TO A WORTHY DISCIPLE. OTHERWISE YOU WILL GO TO HELL". RAMANUJA WITH GREAT EXCITEMENT AND ANXIETY GOT THE MANTRA AND STARTED GOING BACK TO SRIRANGAM. WHILE HE WAS WALKING THINKING OF WHAT HE HEARD, ALL OF A SUDDEN HE HAD A FEELING AND WANTED THIS MANTRA TO BE KNOWN TO ONE AND ALL. SINCE HIS LOVE FOR HUMANITY WAS UNBOUNDED, "HE WANTED THAT EVERY MAN SHOULD ENJOY THE ETERNAL BLISS OF LORD NARAYANA AND ATTAIN SALVATION. SO RAMANUJA CLIMBED ON TO THE VIMANAM OF THE THIRUKOTTIYUR TEMPLE, AND CALLED WHOMSOEVER (SIC) WAS INTERESTED TO LEARN THE DIVINE MANTRA. HE THEN SAID THE MEANING OF THE THIRUMANTRAM TO ALL THOSE WHO WERE INTERESTED, REGARDLESS OF CASTE OR CREED. WHEN NAMBI CAME TO KNOW OF THIS, HE BECAME FURIOUS. HE RUSHED TO RAMANUJA AND ENQUIRED WHY HE TOLD THIS AGAINST THE PROMISE HE HAD GIVEN. RAMANUJA REPLIED THAT BY TELLING THIS DIVINE MANTRA ONLY HE WILL GO TO HELL BUT THE ENTIRE HUMANITY WILL ATTAIN SALVATION. NAMBI WAS VERY MUCH PLEASED WITH RAMANUJA AND FOUND OUT THAT HE HAD A VERY LARGE HEART FULL OF COMPASSION. HE EMBRACED RAMANUJA AND BLESSED HIM. (M. VENKATARAMAN. OP. CIT. (PP. 13-14). UNKNOWN. KINDLE EDITION.")

This, too, is what I have learned in this seventh incarnation as a result of researching, editing, and republishing Yogananda's *Praecepta*. In spite of imprecations and threats of 'hell fire' I found it important to share Yogananda's teachings, including his Kriya teachings.

But in-so-doing I discovered the darker side of Yogananda, which was discussed in the previous chapter. The name given a swami at time of *sannyas* vows has more than a spiritual import. It is also a way for society at large to be able to identify a swami who is behaving badly.

And that is the startling turn that my research has taken. But this time I am spiritually more mature and find myself 'trucking on' my journey with joy. Yogananda has said, "TO BE FIT FOR SELF-REALIZATION, ONE MUST BE FEARLESS."

You cannot have half of God

Swami Satyeswaranandaji shares an insight in his *The Bible in the Light of Kriya Yoga* that is astounding!

"As God is Love, so is He also Terrible. To the devotional seeker, God is Love.

"But true seekers of Truth prepare themselves to accept God as He is. God is the equilibrium state of Breath, beyond all   classes of force, energy, and speed . . .

"The equilibrium state of pure Consciousness is an undifferentiated state of Consciousness. This is the true form of God, the Most High, who is truly Detachment, Terrible and absolutely Indifferent to results, rewards, or good and bad.

"When the true seeker of Truth and not he who seeks love or mystic power, in fact, realizes this Terrible, Indifferent, Detached character of God, he attains Fearlessness, or absolute Freedom, because there is no more extreme state than this state of Consciousness.

"Once the seeker attains the Realization of the Terrible state of Consciousness, there is no state or situation that can threaten him with fear.

"It is thus essential to realize the Terrible aspect, or the Detachment aspect, of the Lord to attain absolute Freedom. Only then can the seeker truly realize God, or attain eternal Liberation. (The Holy Bible in the Light of Kriya Yoga, p. 141; The Sanskrit Classics, San Diego, Ca.)

Whatever else I learned of Yogananda in this seven volume publishing and editing exercise, I learned more about myself than about him. And for sure I learned that the drama he played -- he played well. My role should have been then, as it is now, to play my role with equanimity always 'looking within' (to paraphrase Sriyukteswar "let us hie homeward within") for answers rather than stumbling on the role someone else is assigned.

Called unto holiness -- ogres and augers

"And Jesus asked, who do you say that I am?" (Mark 8:29)

In my linguistic studies I found the primary influence of Sanskrit on English, for instance "Om" is the origin of the "amen" of the Jews and Christians, and of "amin" of Muslims. I found the interesting linguistic formation "perfect peace" in Isaiah is formed by doubling 'shalom.' Likewise I find that English 'omnipresence' is formed in Sanskrit (so I'm told) by doubling 'omni.'

Though I find no linguistic support for my belief that today's 'ogre' comes from Sanskrit 'auger,' I want to make a point. For purposes of finding a way to 'rehab' Yogananda's image, I shall assume the theory, torpedoes be damned!

The word 'ogre' implies someone ugly both in physical features and in behavior. I have heard 'ogre' defined as a 'hominid.'

The Sanskrit 'auger' has an entirely different meaning. I conflate the two words because they are pronounced the same. Baba Hari Das explains:

"Aughar is the word for an ascetic who leads an "awkward" life. Because of his strange behavior and awkward life pattern, this siddha was called Aughar Baba." (DASS, BABA HARI. HARIAKHAN BABA: KNOWN, UNKNOWN (KINDLE LOCATIONS 756-757). KINDLE EDITION.)

By strange and awkward Dass speaks further of this *siddha*:

"AUGHAR IS ACTUALLY A HIGH STAGE IN A YOGI'S LIFE WHEN ALL RULES ARE FINISHED. IT IS THE HIGHEST DISCIPLINE, WITHOUT ANY WORLDLY DISCIPLINE. CONTRARY TO ACCEPTED PRACTICE FOR RELIGIOUS SECTS, AUGHARS HAVE NO RULES FOR EATING, SLEEPING, CLEANLINESS, OR WEARING PARTICULAR ROBES. FOR THEM THERE IS NO DIFFERENCE BETWEEN THE WATER IN THE GUTTER AND THE SACRED WATER FROM THE GANGES RIVER. FOR THEM THERE IS NO DIFFERENCE BETWEEN A DIET OF PURE FRUIT AND VEGETABLES AND THE DECAYED FLESH OF DEAD ANIMALS. THEY ARE ABOVE "GOOD AND BAD"". (DASS, BABA HARI. HARIAKHAN BABA: KNOWN, UNKNOWN (KINDLE LOCATIONS 757-761). KINDLEEDITION.)

Do you remember when Yogananda describes being able to eat a fistful of rotting rice without ill effect, and then, seeing his childhood comrades repulsed, he successfully shoved a handful into the mouth of one of them. His childhood friend obliged by promptly vomiting.

So is this an indication that Mukunda was or had attained the high state of *siddha*? I have no idea: and to be clear about it, it's not up to me to explain (or 'rehab') Yogananda and his image. But for those who have already on Facebook kindly baptized me with the designation of 'POS,' for examining these things, I shall proceed as if I were the *siddha*.

Speaking of 'POS,' I have found descriptions of saintly lives by various swamis that challenge societal norms. Swami Jnanananda Giri (*Transcendent Journey*) speaks lovingly of a reclusive saint who occasionally produced a ball of feces and promptly ate it, as if it were nourishing. Baba Hari Dass speaks similarly of *Augur Baba*

"ONCE WHEN PEOPLE WERE SURROUNDING HIM, HE PASSED A STOOL AND BEGAN TO EAT IT. FOR MOST IT WAS A VERY AWKWARD MOMENT, BUT ONE MAN THERE WAS A SCHOLAR OF SANSKRIT AND HE SAID THAT THE MAN WAS AN ASCETIC OF THE AUGHAR STAGE. FROM THAT TIME, PEOPLE BEGAN TO CALL HIM AUGHAR BABA." (DASS, BABA HARI. HARIAKHAN BABA: KNOWN, UNKNOWN (KINDLE LOCATIONS 770-772). KINDLE EDITION.)

Sri M (that living Christ of India) speaks in his two volumes of autobiographical material of saints who behave or dress or marry (or not) but always he speaks with respect and acknowledgement of their high spiritual attainment. He gives a graphic account at (I believe) the *Manikarnika Ghat* of fellowshipping with a high-souled being who disguised himself as a dirty madman. Sri M could see the saint in his true manifestation, regal bearing, shining with the radiance of the Divine. A young American girl called out to the saint telling him she believed him to be her guru. He had hidden himself from her view; he responded by demanding that she rip off her shirt so he could (censored censored) her. Sri M watched with interest as she ran off quite quickly; scared by the prospects of this quick turn of events.

Unsurprisingly and actually unnecessarily to Sri M the saint explained he was testing her.

Srimati Nerode states that when Yogananda used the commode in the mobile car, Durga Ma used to clean his bottom. (Reread #19 and #20 in Appendix Reference). Some of my FB friends thought this was a bad sign of some kind. But notice Swami Shuddhanandaji's description of the guru's behavior towards Baba Lokenath Brahmachari.

"[LOKENATH] SAID, "GURUDEV WOULD ALWAYS BE ALERT SO THAT WE DID NOT NEED TO MOVE OUR BODIES WHILE WE WERE SEATED AT MEDITATION DURING THIS FASTING. WE WERE NOT ALLOWED TO MOVE, EVEN WHILE ATTENDING TO THE CALL OF NATURE. LIKE A LOVING MOTHER, HE WOULD WASH AWAY URINE OR STOOL AND CARRY US TO A CLEAN PLACE. HE WOULD THEN REMOVE THE STOOL, THROW IT A DISTANCE AWAY, AND THEN FINALLY CLEAN THE WHOLE PLACE."" (SHUDDHAANANDAA BRAHMACHARI. THE INCREDIBLE LIFE OF A HIMALAYAN YOGI: THE TIMES, TEACHINGS AND LIFE OF

LIVING SHIVA: BABA LOKENATH BRAHMACHARI (P. 31). LOKENATH DIVINE LIFE MISSION, KOLKATA, INDIA. KINDLE EDITION.)

Shuddhanandaji writes on with a paean of joy to the merits and usefulness of a guru, pointing out that

"FROM OUTSIDE, THE SATGURU PUSHES US INWARD. THE SATGURU ALSO GUIDES FROM WITHIN." (IBID., P. 33).

Was this Yogananda? If so the crucial question is what has the guru done for me? Satyeswaranandaji comments in one of his books (I think it's in *The Holy Bible in the Light of Kriya Yoga*) "the yogi succeeds to the extent of the guru's obedience to the Divine."

What Has the Guru Done for Me Lately?

Certainly most of Yogananda's original male disciples speak gratefully of the role he played in their spiritual growth. Probably Swami Kriyananda is one of the most eloquent of such writers. Durga Ma and Sister Gyanamataji likewise speak highly of him. Gyanamataji seems best to have seen past his role of blustery bravado and perceived the divinity within.

Likewise I have spoken in this book about some of my encounters with Yogananda in this lifetime, omitting some of the more recent ones. I say about those experiences what I say about all spiritual experiences: of themselves they convey no sainthood, though for sure much good is conveyed.

There are more written accounts of Yogananda's behavior that speak eloquently to his spiritual attainment. You may recall that a young monk acknowledged that upon meeting Ananda Moyi Ma, she slapped him for the thought that he admitted was running through his mind.

Yogananda, on the other hand, writes of his first meeting with her:

"The woman saint glanced in our direction; she alit from her car and walked toward us. "Father, you have come!" With these fervent words she put her arm around my neck and her head on my shoulder. Mr. Wright, to whom I had just remarked that I did not know the saint, was hugely enjoying this extraordinary demonstration of welcome. The eyes of the one hundred chelas were also fixed with some surprise on the affectionate tableau. (Paramhansa Yogananda. Autobiography of a Yogi (Reprint of the Philosophical library 1946 First Edition) (p. 281). Crystal Clarity Publishers - A. Kindle Edition.)

By this time several years had elapsed since Swami Dhirananda had split from Yogananda for his sexual behavior. Yet during this time Sri Nerode had been loyally confronting Yogananda and recommending marriage as a way to save himself from himself. (As discussed by Srimati, referenced earlier.)

The insights of two other later Indian disciples, Swamis Satchidananda Giri and Bidyananda Giri are wonderful because they document Yogananda's appearances to them (after his 1952 departure from this world) at times when they were in need of guidance. I commend these two autobiographies to you, "My Struggle for Self-Realization," Swami Satchidanandaji, and "Jeevansmriti," Swami Bidyanandaji.

It's important, I think, to point out that in-spite-of the history of difficult personal interactions experienced by Swami Atmanandaji and das Gupta with Yogananda, both referred to him as "that God-man."

A Final Word

Do Yogananda's actions rise to the level of reducing the *karmic* load of those around him? The usual understanding of the guru-disciple relationship is that in all things, the guru is always the guru. Remember Gyanamata's admitted acknowledgement of this relationship by being quiet and looking away from Yogananda when in his presence.

On the other hand neither Bettelu nor the Nerodes were in a guru-disciple relationship with Yogananda. In Yogananda's mind as reported in his East-West magazine, he would have Yogoda members believe that Sri Nerode was his *chela*. Remember Durga Ma speaks to Yogananda about Teresa Newmann taking bad habits of devotees upon herself:

"One day I asked Master, "Sir, I read an article about Therese Newmann wherein she took upon her own body the bad habits of priests, etc. Some days her breath and

BODY OOZED THE SMELL OF CIGARETTE SMOKE OR LIQUOR, ALTHOUGH SHE HADN'T TAKEN EITHER ONE OF THESE ITEMS. COULD YOU PLEASE EXPLAIN THIS TO ME." HIS ANSWER WAS, "THOSE WHO HELP OTHER SOULS, DO NOT ONLY TAKE OTHERS PHYSICAL DISEASES BUT ALSO TAKES ON SUCH HABITS AS EATING, DRINKING, JEALOUSIES, ANGER, GREED AND ALL OTHER PSYCHOLOGICAL TENDENCIES AS WELL. THEY SOMETIMES, THE HEALER, HAS TO ACT OUT THOSE PARTICULAR TENDENCIES IN THEIR OWN BODIES OR ACTIONS." MASTER INTIMATED THAT EACH CONSECUTIVE DISCIPLE THAT CAME TO HIM HAD DIFFERENT HABITS AND IN ORDER TO HELP HIM OR HER BREAK THAT HABIT, HE USED HIMSELF AS THE SHOCK ABSORBER AND TOOK UPON HIMSELF THE CONSEQUENCES OF THE ACTIONS OR DISEASES, ETC." (A PARAMHANSA YOGANANDA TRILOGY OF DIVINE LOVE)

Did Yogananda see himself somehow taking on someone's karma by attempting to rape them or in any other wise "acting badly" towards them? Damn if I know.

I end this book with an insightful observation by Baba Lokenath. In many ways his insight mirrors Krishna's remark in the *Bhagavad-Gita* that God is the author of all action.

"THE WOMAN SAID, "BABA, I AM NOT ABLE TO PARDON MYSELF FOR ALL MY EVIL DOINGS. THE FAITH AND LOVE THAT MY HUSBAND HAS FOR ME ADDS TO THE FIRE OF MY INNER AGONY WHICH I CAN NEITHER EXPRESS NOR ENDURE. SOMETIMES I FEEL THAT I SHOULD COMMIT SUICIDE TO END THIS AGONIZING STATE IN MY LIFE."

"BABA, THE DIVINE PHYSICIAN, CONSOLED THE UNHAPPY WOMAN, "HAVE YOU EVER THOUGHT ABOUT WHO IT IS THAT MOTIVATES YOU FROM WITHIN TO DO RIGHT OR WRONG? I AM THE ONE SITTING IN THE VERY CORE OF YOUR HEART. IT IS MY WILL ALONE WHICH PLAYS THROUGH YOU. IF THE WILL IS MINE, THEN HOW CAN THE SIN BE YOURS? IF ANYBODY IS TO BE BLAMED IT IS NOT YOU, BUT ME."

"THE YOUNG WOMAN WAS INCREDULOUS. SHE HAD NEVER BEFORE HEARD ANYTHING LIKE THIS. THE GODMAN WHO WAS SMILING SO COMPASSIONATELY NOT ONLY EXONERATED HER, BUT ALSO ASSUMED THE BLAME FOR THE SINS THAT SHE HAD COMMITTED.

"BABA SAID, "YOU WILL NOT UNDERSTAND MY WORDS, BUT ALWAYS KEEP IN MIND THAT YOU ARE NOT A SINNER ANYMORE. YOUR HUSBAND IS A NICE BOY AND HE HAS NO COMPLAINTS AGAINST YOU. HE ONLY WANTS YOU TO BE HAPPY IN LIFE. FROM TODAY, I TAKE TOTAL RESPONSIBILITY FOR YOU BOTH. LEAVE ALL THE THOUGHTS OF SIN AND YOUR PAST WITH ME AND GO BACK HOME TO LEAD A HAPPY MARRIED LIFE. YOU WILL SEE THAT YOU WILL HAVE NO MORE TROUBLES IN LIFE."

"THE WOMAN FELT AS IF SHE HAD BEEN TOUCHED BY MAGIC. THE HEAVINESS OF HER HEART AND MIND DISSOLVED, LEAVING NO TRACE OF HER PAST AGONY. SHE WAS AT PEACE. BATHED IN THE DIVINE GRACE OF BABA, SHE SURRENDERED AT HIS FEET SAYING, "BABA, YOU HAVE SHOWERED ME WITH SO MUCH GRACE. BLESS ME, SO THAT I MAY ALWAYS REMEMBER YOUR KINDNESS AND GRACE BY REMAINING EVER ENGAGED IN DEVOTIONAL SERVICE TO YOUR LOTUS FEET."

"FROM HIS STATE OF SUPREME DIVINITY, BABA DECLARED, "THE ONE IS EVERYWHERE. THERE IS NO SECOND. WHO WILL SHOW KINDNESS TO WHOM? HAVE YOU EVER SEEN A PERSON IN THIS WORLD WHO IS KIND TO HIMSELF? I DO NOT FIND THE EXISTENCE OF ANYTHING OTHER THAN ME IN THIS ENTIRE CREATION. I HAVE TRAVELED IN THE HILLS AND MOUNTAINS, IN THE JUNGLES AND

FORESTS, ALL OVER THE WORLD, BUT COULD ONLY SEE MYSELF. YOU WILL NOT UNDERSTAND WHY I LOVE YOU ALL SO MUCH, WHY I AM SHARING YOUR MISERIES AND UNHAPPINESS."

"THE HUSBAND AND WIFE DRANK THE NECTAR OF BABA'S ETERNAL WORDS. PROSTRATING THEMSELVES AT THE FEET OF THIS LIVING EMBODIMENT OF LOVE AND COMPASSION, THEY TOOK THEIR LEAVE OF BABA WITH HIS WORDS STILL RINGING THE YOUNG WOMAN'S EARS." (SHUDDHAANANDAA BRAHMACHARI. THE INCREDIBLE LIFE OF A HIMALAYAN YOGI: THE TIMES, TEACHINGS AND LIFE OF LIVING SHIVA: BABA LOKENATH BRAHMACHARI (PP. 95-96). LOKENATH DIVINE LIFE MISSION, KOLKATA, INDIA. KINDLE EDITION.)

Om, amen, amin, shanti

APPENDIX REFERENCE

NOTE: This Appendix Reference has been placed on the internet at http://glimpses.us to increase readability. Therefore it is not printed in this edition.

INDEX